Death and Social Media

JACQUI BRAUMAN

Copyright © 2015 Jacqui Brauman

ISBN: 978-0-9945146-2-2

DEDICATION

To my husband, who tolerates my dreams and puts up with my workaholism. It's all for you.

CONTENTS

ACKNOWLEDGMENTS

This book came about after I wrote a research paper for the College of Law as part of my Masters of Applied Law (Wills and Estates). I need to thank Ines Kallweit for her support during the writing of that research paper and her feedback, as well as thanking the College of Law to agreeing to accept the topic.

1 INTRODUCTION

The Internet is changing our lives, and the speed of the change is only going to increase exponentially. In October 2014, the number of phone SIMS cards exceeded the number of people on Earth for the first time. In the next five years, another billion people will become connected to the Internet, primarily via smart phones. This will change our banking and our finance sector, it will change the education industry, and a whole new world of crime will emerge.

With everyone on Earth connected to the Internet, the world becomes a very small place, and the myth of the national state that humans have created will be challenged. The law already cannot keep up, nor can any legislature. Jurisdictional problems will increase, and warrants put out for the arrest of certain cyber criminals will be a token gesture only. Therefore, individuals will need to take more responsibility of their own privacy and digital assets. Or there will have to be international cooperation and conventions on multiple issues.

Practical solutions will need to be developed, since regulated solutions will be outdated by the time they come into existence. This book is seeking just that: educate more people about their digital assets so they can take responsibility for them, and provide a practical solution for estate planning solicitors to help assist clients manage their digital assets before and after death or incapacity. It is important to note the law does not start here from a blank canvas, as existing laws will already partially regulate the issues. Almost all legal systems have rules relating to the transmission of property on death, under the name of wills and testament law, succession and probate. The law regulating the procedure to wind up the deceased's estate is a separate branch of law gain, usually called executry or administration.

A key issue is how far digital assets fit within existing legal paradigms, and whether new law is needed. Generally assets only fall into the estate of a deceased if they are "property". Some digital assets are too evanescent to be property. Also, digital assets are controlled by online businesses and custodians, and understanding the terms of service agreements is another key issue to dealing with these online businesses.

This book will consider a number of the most popular online businesses which people use today, and in which they generally think they have a digital asset or something to control and recover. Each chapter will consider a different online business or custodian and its user agreement, along with some practical steps that can be taken for estate planning. In the later chapters, this book will review what an estate asset is, and whether digital assets will fit within such a definition. Then some general definitions for digital assets will be proposed, along with some suggested clauses of Wills and Powers of Attorney.

2 ITUNES

David is a 22-year-old student. He is in his final Honours year of a science degree. He lives in a single bedroom unit near the university, and works at Donut King in the local shopping centre. The money he earns is spent mainly on going out with his friends, because his parents pay his rent. He likes going to see live bands play in pubs and little underground basements. He and his friends like grunge, heavy metal and some electronica music.

Rarely does David drive home to see his parents in Gippsland, but he decides to drive home on the Mother's Day weekend. It is a wet Friday evening when he leaves the campus, having swapped his weekend shift at Donut King with someone else. The roads are slippery, and he gets confused by the lights reflecting on the wet road. Speed also plays a factor, the police will later tell his parents, but in fact he was sitting right on the speed limit. He should have been going a bit slower when he hit the corner, as he understeers and ploughs into a tree. He doesn't die instantly, but tragically bleeds out as emergency crews are trying to get to him.

He had been fairly meticulous, for a young man. When he turned 18, at the off-the-cuff suggestion of his father, he had taken out a life insurance policy and made a Will. He had appointed his parents as his executors and he had left everything to his younger brother.

David's younger brother Hugh is 20-years-old. It takes a few weeks before he is ready to go through David's room at their parents' house. His parents had arranged for a removals company to clean out David's unit and bring all his belongings back home. They were all still in boxes in his old bedroom.

Hugh goes through David's laptop first. There is an extensive music collection in iTunes, along with lots of downloaded video, both TV episodes and movies. Hugh goes into the account settings and de-authorises all the other computers that can share files bought through David's account. He does this because David has already shared with the maximum amount of people that he can share with, and Hugh wants to be one of those people. So Hugh enters his own Apple ID to authorise his iTunes account to share. What Hugh didn't think was that David's friends have now lost a large amount of music from their libraries, as they are no longer authorised to play the songs that David had downloaded.

Now that all the files are shared, over the following months Hugh forgets what he has downloaded himself, and what music and video he is sharing through David's account. Hugh regularly uses some "ripper" software to rip a lot of music out of iTunes and into different formats for non-compatible devices.

About two years after David his died, his parents insist that Hugh clean up David's room somewhat, so that only the important things are kept and to discard the rest. Hugh decides that most of David's electronic devices are obsolete - they are already too old and Hugh has later models. Before arranging for the laptop to be recycled, Hugh methodically goes through the laptop and shuts down accounts and wipes the memory of the computer.

Hugh is later annoyed that a substantial amount of music in his iTunes library is gone. He did not realise that you don't own the music you download on iTunes, but you are instead licensed to use it. When Hugh deleted David's account, all the licensed music and video that he had paid for was revoked and gone. Luckily Hugh had been ripping out the music that he particularly liked and used in other formats, but David had spent a significant amount of money with iTunes over the years and it was all just gone.

Legal

The Terms and Conditions of use of Apple accounts, including iTunes, App Store, iBooks and iCloud, are available at the bottom of their websites: https://www.apple.com/legal/internet-services/itunes/. Their Terms and Conditions are based on the country of domicile, so Australian courts do have jurisdiction over an

Apple account.

When a user signs up for iTunes Services they enter into an agreement with Apple Pty Limited (ABN 46 002 510 054), which permits the user to access, purchase or rent digital content. It is a breach of the Terms for a user to reveal their account information (user name and password) to anyone else, for security and privacy reasons.

There are means to submit materials to iTunes to be available to the public. By doing so, the user grants Apple a worldwide, royalty-free, nonexclusive license to use such materials.

The products on iTunes can be shared over 5 devices, and burnt onto another device or disc up to 7 times. The terms suggest that termination of an account does not affect the products that have already been acquired, but it will limit being able to share and authorise other computers and devices to use the products.

The Terms and Conditions are silent on whether the account is transferrable or whether the licence to use the products is exclusive (other than the limited shares permitted). The Terms and Conditions do not contemplate death.

The likely result on death is that the service agreement between Apple and the user is terminated. In the event of termination of an account, the Terms and Conditions expressly states that the products acquired will not be affected, but it unlikely that other computers or devices can be added to the licence thereafter.

Apple should also be informed of the death of the user, so that no further purchases can accidentally be made by the account, and charged to a credit card that should no longer be used. Correspondence can be forwarded to Apple at PO Box A2629, Sydney South NSW 1235.

Practical

Practically, this means that if family members want to retain the contents of their deceased loved one's iTunes account, then they should burn it onto another device. Even if the content of the account is already shared with other family members, with updates and the fast changing pace of technology, it could be a few short years before the content may be outdated or incompatible let alone the original digital device.

3 GOOGLE

Harry and his wife Patricia have been married for 20 years. They are an active young family with three young boys in primary school. Harry is a self-employed online marketing consultant who earns enough that Patricia doesn't have to work, and also has flexible hours so that he can spend a lot of time with his family. Their family home is full of love and laughter, a lot of rough and tumble activity from the boys, and plenty of outdoor activities.

Harry still plays B-grade Australian Rules football on Saturday mornings during the winter season. Despite being very fit for his age, he suffers from a major heart attack during a game and dies in hospital later.

It is such an unexpected tragedy that the whole community, especially the football team, rally around Patricia and the boys. In their grief, they are able to manage by all the support they are shown. There is always someone coming around bringing them food, and doing a bit of housework for them, and making them talk and think about things other than the huge hole in their lives - Harry.

Harry has provided very well for Patricia. The mortgage is paid off, and she has a $500,000 nest egg from his life insurance. But after a few months, she decides that she needs to work, for her own sanity. She decides to do an online course in adult training and education to get her back into the workforce. She diligently starts studying and is on her laptop doing some reading or writing for her course most days. She believes it's also good that the boys see her doing this.

About six months after Harry died, Patricia gets a surprise email from Google that his account has been inactive for 6 months, so it had triggered the Inactive Account Manager setting that he had recorded. At some stage, when this facility first became available by Google, Harry must have set it up to forward all his Google accounts to Patricia if his account was inactive for 6 months.

Patricia starts getting all his gmail. She now has access to his Google Drive, where he had kept most of his work. All his Contacts are now available to Patricia, and his Google+ Pages and Google+ Photos. She goes through the photos that he had, and there are many of her that she had never seen. He had a lot of family photos that he had taken on his mobile and uploaded into Google+ Photos which she now had access to.

When she was about to close down his Google+ Pages for his business, she pauses. She wondered if she could use his contacts to continue on a similar business. She could provide adult training for small businesses in online marketing. She decided to look through all his work in Google Drive. There were a substantial amount of systems and work flows that he had utilised for himself that she thought she could re-purpose into a course.

She was very grateful that Harry had been so organised - he was organised in the systems he set up in his business, and organised enough to set up Google's Inactive Account Manager. If he had not authorised her to have access to his accounts and start receiving everything after 6 months, then she would have lost all the photos he had, and all the work he had done. Patricia quietly thanked him, her heart aching, but she realised she had loved the right man who really had looked after her as best he could.

Legal

A user can create a Google account for personal use, or they can have a Google account assigned to them be an administrator, such as an employer or educational institution. The Terms of Service can be found from most of their sites: https://www.google.com.au/intl/en/policies/terms/regional.html.

When a user creates a Google account, the other party to the agreement is Google Inc of 1600 Amphitheatre Parkway, Mountain View, CA 94043, United States. The Terms of Service do not specifically state the jurisdiction that applies, but it is assumed that Californian (USA) law would apply.

Some of the services offered to a Google account holder include being able to upload, store, send and receive content. The Terms of Service confirm that ownership of any intellectual property is retained by the user, but you give Google a worldwide licence to use, host, store, reproduce, communicate, publish or publicly display that content. This licence continues even after the user cancels their account.

An account can be terminated by either party at any time. Google confirms their belief in the ownership of a user's data, and states that a reasonable notice and chance will be given to get the information out of the Google account.

In 2013, Google implemented an Inactive Account Manager policy. An account user can nominate whether their content is deleted, or whether it is forwarded to a trusted person after a chosen period of time: 3, 6, 9 or 12 months. When Inactive Account Manager is enabled, it reminds you every 3 months or so that it is enabled. Before the system takes action, a text message will be sent to the user's linked mobile phone and a message sent to the registered secondary email address.

As death or the transferability of an account is not mentioned in the Terms of Service, the question arises as to what happens to a Google account and all its various aspects (gmail, Google +, Blogger, YouTube, Google Drive, Analytics and other services). Google's privacy policy is one of its priorities, with its two-step authentication process and other measures, it is likely that if a user doesn't nominate an Inactive Account Manager themselves then it will be very difficult for a family member to establish any authority to access the account. A request regarding a deceased user's account can be submitted here: https://support.google.com/accounts/contact/deceased?hl=en.

Practical

Practically, everyone with a Google account should implement the Inactive Account Manager feature. But if someone has passed away without having done so, it would be prudent for the executor or family member to try logging into the Google account on the deceased person's device. Often, passwords are saved in the computer. If the account can be accessed, then download all the content from Google Drive and deactivate parts of the account that are not needed. You may also be able to redirect all the emails from the gmail account. Accessing someone else's account without their permission (because they have died) is not ideal and could even be in breach of the terms of service of the Google account, but practically this is often the quickest and easiest way to get access. If the family do not have the password and cannot otherwise access the account, they would need to contact Google to get access and this may or may not be granted.

4 MICROSOFT/HOTMAIL

In the previous chapter, with Harry and Patricia, if Harry had been with Hotmail and had a Microsoft account instead of Google here's what would have happened:

After Harry's death, Patricia would have still gone back to study. But 6 months after Harry's death, she would not have got any email from Microsoft as with Google. She would have had to wonder what happened to all Harry's emails and work that he kept online. If the thought had occurred to her, she could have contacted Microsoft. However, if the thought hadn't occurred to her within 12 months of Harry dying, everything in Harry's Hotmail account and Microsoft account would have been deleted, because it had been inactive for too long.

If Patricia had contacted Microsoft, she would have then had to send a certified copy of the death certificate, a certified copy of the marriage certificate, a certified copy of the Will, a certified copy of her photo ID, along with Harry's full identification details. If all the documentation was adequate, Microsoft would put everything in Harry's online accounts onto a data DVD and sent it to Patricia.

All Harry's accounts would then be deleted.

Microsoft does not make accounts available to anyone else, and they do not transfer the accounts to a new user. They make the material available to the family, and then delete it, or delete it after 12 months anyway.

Legal

The Terms of Use for an account with Microsoft for one of its various online products or services are available depending on your domicile: http://www.microsoft.com/australia/legal/te

<u>rms-conditions.aspx</u>.

The other entity for the agreement is not mentioned, and nor is the jurisdiction that applies. In the Arbitration and Dispute Resolution policy, King County, Seattle is the preferred jurisdiction, but it also states that proceedings can be brought in the county where the complainant lives. The policy only contemplates USA citizens.

A user must keep their username and password secure, and report unauthorised access immediately. Interestingly, the Terms of Service state that a user may use another person's account with their permission. This implies that a user can authorise a third party to operate their account.

Similar licences are provided to Microsoft as to Google for any content uploaded onto Microsoft platforms, except that the licence for Microsoft to use such content is terminated once the content is removed from the account. This implies that if the account is terminated, the content is also removed.

The Terms of Use do not mention death or incapacity, but a further search reveals a

Microsoft Next of Kin policy. There is a long list of information that must be provided to msrecord@microsoft.com or by fax to (425) 708-7851 or by mail to Next of Kin, One Microsoft Way, Redmond, WA 98052 USA. The Next of Kin process does not allow account access, will not change passwords, and will not support the account. The account will be closed and the contents in the account will be forwarded to the authenticated next of kin by way of a data DVD.

Practical

As with Google, it would be prudent for the executor or family member to try logging into the Microsoft account on the deceased person's device. Often, passwords are saved in the computer. If the account can be accessed, then download all the content that can be downloaded. You may also be able to redirect all the emails from the hotmail account, but remember that the account is still likely to be deleted after it is inactive for 12 months. Accessing someone else's account without their permission (because they have died) is not ideal, but practically this is often the quickest and easiest way to get access. If the family do not have the password and cannot otherwise access the account, they would need to contact Microsoft as outlined above to get access, and this may or may not be granted

5 FACEBOOK

Amanda was beautiful. Maybe not classically beautiful, but she had a spark in her that could been seen by others from miles away. She had dark brown hair, dark brown eyes, and she was an average height for a sixteen-year-old. She got average grades, and enjoyed lunch breaks with her friends at school more than any other time. She played netball for a local club on Saturdays and trained two nights per week. She had a job a McDonalds, and had had a couple of boyfriends over the years. Her parents were happily married, and she had a younger brother. Despite how average she looked on paper, it was the spark that drew people to her. She had a confident, comfortable nature and radiated energy.

It was a shock for everyone, when Amanda was the third girl in three weeks to commit suicide. The small community reeled, and the police reported that they had foiled a fourth girl from completing a suicide pact that the girls had all made. Amanda had snuck out of her house in the early hours of the morning on her final day of life, while the whole town was asleep. She had tiptoed past her parents' bedroom where they slept soundly, unknowing that their beautiful daughter was so troubled. She had made her way to the railway tracks in time for the early morning freight train, and had stepped out of the shadows straight into its path. The driver was left devastated.

During her short life, Amanda had accumulated over 400 friends on Facebook. She had uploaded lots of selfies and pictures of friends, and had regularly communicated publicly in her Facebook feed.

In the first week whilst her family were grieving, even before her parents had been able to collect Amanda's body from the coroner to be able to bury her, there was a flood of grief and well-wishes posted onto

Amanda's Facebook page. Since her parents' lives had shut down that week, neither were checking Facebook, so neither of them saw the outpouring in their own feeds.

But Amanda's grandmother, Cathy, was also friends with Amanda on Facebook, and she was still checking her feeds throughout the days. She was disgusted when she saw the first post:

"You did the world a favour. You should have killed yourself earlier".

Cathy couldn't delete the post from Amanda's feed, because it wasn't posted on her own page. She didn't know what to do, but hoped that enough new posts by Amanda's friends would push this post far enough down that Amanda's parents wouldn't see it. But hope isn't a strategy. Instead, Amanda's friends engaged with the troll and began a long abusive fight that lasted for days.

Cathy went to see Amanda's parents at their home later on the first day after the post, when there were already 23 comments backwards and forwards between the troll and Amanda's friends. The distress pushed

Amanda's mother over the edge, and she broke down and had to be hospitalised.

Amanda's father tried to log into Amanda's Facebook page, but couldn't work out or retrieve the password. He tried contacting Facebook, but he had no proof of death, as Amanda's death certificate had not yet arrived. Also, because Amanda was a minor, she didn't have a Will to appoint a legal personal representative.

Amanda's father took days to contact a real person at Facebook who was actually in Australia that he could explain the situation to. He had to prove he was Amanda's father, and he had to provide copies of newspaper articles about Amanda's death until he could later forward on a copy of the death certificate when it arrived.

Finally, he was given the option of shutting the page down completely or leaving a memorial page. He considered that it would be nice for her friends to still have access to Amanda's photos and be able to be reminded of her, but the ongoing posts by the troll swayed him the other way and he decided to shut the page down. They lost a lot of the online record that Amanda had catalogued over the years, all because of an anonymous hate-monger, and the difficulty to shut the person down.

Legal

Facebook's terms and policies can be found at the bottom of the ads and boxes on the right side of the screen: https://www.facebook.com/policies. For users outside the USA or Canada, the other party to the agreement to use Facebook Services is Facebook Ireland Limited. Despite this, for any dispute arising from the use of Facebook, users submit to the jurisdiction of the US District Court for the Northern District of California or a state court located in San Mateo County.

The data controller for all non-USA/Canadian based users can be contacted at: Facebook Ireland Ltd., 4 Grand Canal Square, Grand Canal Harbour, Dublin 2 Ireland or online: https://www.facebook.com/help/contact/17 3545232710000. The Facebook Australia Support phone number is 001-650-543-4800.

Facebook offers a Download My Data capability, so that any user can log into their page and download a copy of everything they have posted to Facebook, including posts, photos, videos, messages and chat conversations, info from the About section, and more. This could be a useful tool to use before deleting an account.

When a user deletes an account, Facebook deletes everything that the user has posted, including photos, posts and status updates.

Facebook has also recently added the ability for a user to nominate if they want their account memorialised or permanently deleted if they die, and to select a Legacy Contact if they want their account memorialised. No one can log into a memorialised account, and if a Legacy Contact isn't nominated, then the account cannot be changed (including privacy settings, etc). A Legacy Contact can only add new friends, but not delete old friends. A Legacy Contact can respond to posts, but cannot alter old posts or delete offensive posts. If a Legacy Contact is nominated, a user can also select whether they want the Legacy Contact to have the ability to Download My Data.

Only Facebook friends can be added as a Legacy Contact, and only Facebook friends can contact Facebook about the death of a user. Once a Facebook friend is verified by Facebook as a family member of a deceased user, they can request the removal of a user's account or the memorialisation of an account if the user hasn't selected an option themselves.

Practical

Practically, everyone with a Facebook account should implement the Legacy Contact feature. But if someone has passed away without having done so, it would be prudent for the executor or family member to try logging into the Facebook account on the deceased person's device to activate the Download My Data. This will ensure all photos and other uploads are retrieved and not lost. the sooner an account can be memorialised or shut down, the better. In Amanda's case, once her page was memorialised, a troll that was not already a Friend, could not post onto her page. The problem would arise if the troll was a Friend of Amanda, and could continue posting on her page after it was memorialised, since the Legacy Contact could still not delete those troll comments. But there are ways of reporting a Facebook user for their behaviour, and they could be penalised for breaching the terms of service of their own account.

6 TWITTER

Bridget started her party hire business with a focus on children's parties, since she was a mother with young children herself, and couldn't find all the things she needed quickly and easily in the one location. She built the business up over 10 years, with a focus to sell. She built up a strong business Twitter account with tens of thousands of followers. Her Twitter account brings her lots of business, as she regularly puts photos of different party set up ideas that are retweeted. It worked like an extended word of mouth marketing tool so that she was able to expand nationally.

When she decided that her business was big enough, and that it was valuable enough to sell, Bridget contacted a broker to put the business on the market and find her a buyer. A big part of the value of the business is the network Bridget has developed, and she agrees that her website and her Twitter account will be included as the intellectual property of the business in the sale.

Soon, a buyer is found. A contract is entered into and everything is proceeding to a settlement in 30 days.

But Bridget falls and hits her head. Not thinking of it, she doesn't go to the doctor, since it was just foolishness on her part. But two days later, she dies of a sudden brain aneurism.

Her family are trying to grieve, but her solicitor and broker are in panic mode. The purchaser of the business wants it to proceed. They are a bit patient, considering Bridget's death, but they want Bridget's legal personal representative to finish it off within another 30 days. The solicitor impresses on Bridget's husband how important it is to complete this contract. Most of it is already done - all that is needed is the business name transfer and the transfer of the Twitter account.

No one but Bridget was able to use the Twitter account. No one has the log in details.

The purchaser threatens to walk away from the contract, claiming Bridget's husband has breached it because they were unable to complete. The broker calms the situation down.

After a few days of panic, the solicitor gets Bridget's husband to bring her laptop into his office. Bridget's laptop has all her passwords saved into the background of it, as she was able to automatically log in each time instead of having to enter the password. All that is needed is an IT expert that can recover the password from the laptop's memory. The solicitor hires one and gets him to come to the office.

Half an hour later, the IT guy has worked his magic and has recovered the password to Bridget's Twitter account from the laptop's memory. The sale contract is able to be completed, and Bridget's estate gets an extra $500,000 straight away, instead of having this contract fall over and have to try to sell the business later once it is already starting to fail without Bridget's magic. This way, the asset is maximised for the estate, and the value of the business doesn't decline without Bridget at the helm.

The crisis could have been averted if Bridget kept a comprehensive list of log-ins and passwords with her Will or other important documents.

Legal

Twitter users enter into a binding contract subject to Twitter Terms of Service, the latest version of which can always be found at: www.twitter.com.tos/. For any non-USA citizens using Twitter, the entity with which we contract is Twitter International Company, an Irish company, with its registered office at The Academy, 42 Pearse Street, Dublin 2, Ireland.

Twitter has an Inactive Account Policy, under which they permanently remove an account if it has been inactive for 6 months. A user can also deactivate their account, which will lead to permanent deletion 30 days thereafter.

A user can download an archive of their data from Twitter by selecting Request Your Archive from the Settings menu. Before a deceased's account is deactivated, an archive could also be requested.

By searching in Twitter's Help Centre, they have instructions for a person authorised to act on the behalf of the estate or with a verified immediate family member of the deceased to have an account deactivated. On receipt of the request, Twitter will email the person who submitted the request to get more information, including ID, and a death certificate.

Rather than removing an account, the family of a deceased user can request that certain images or video be removed in certain circumstances.

Twitter will work with the person authorised to act on behalf of the estate of a deceased person, or with a verified immediate family member of the deceased, to have an account deactivated.

The following information should be sent by mail to Twitter to process the account deactivation:

the username of the Twitter account (@username or <u>twitter.com/username</u>)

- a copy of the deceased user's death certificate
- a copy of your government issued ID (drivers licence or other photographic ID preferred)
- a signed statement (preferably a statutory declaration) including:
  - your first and last name
  - your email address
  - your current contact information
  - your relationship to the deceased user or their estate
  - action requested ("please deactivate the Twitter account)
  - a brief description of the details that evidence this account belongs to the deceased, if the name on the account does not match the death certificate, and
  - a link to an online obituary or a copy of an obituary from a newspaper

The postal address is:

Twitter Inc, c/- Trust & Safety, 1355 Market Street, Suite 900, San Francisco, CA 94103, USA.

Twitter can also be contacted at privacy@twitter.com.

Practical

Bridget's case was not that unusual. When someone dies, there is usually 6-8 weeks before the death certificate arrives, which is often the minimum requirement for proof of death from Twitter or other custodian businesses. Bridget's account was also a business account, not a personal account, so it could be transferred by handing over the account details. The new owner would then log in, change the password, and change account details. Generally, a personal account has little value and would not need to be transferred, but the family would often want a download of all the data before the account was deleted. If the password is known, then a download can be effected by the family members logging in, and then the account can be deleted later once the death certificate arrives and authority is established with Twitter to do so.

7 EBAY

John and Tracey had opened their eBay account in 2005. It was linked to Tracey's email address, and John and Tracey both used the same eBay account for their various purchases and occasional sales over the years. Tracey bought dresses from China and cheap electronic gadgets, and John bought die-cast model cars, shoes and cycling gear. They had well over 100 transactions and were rated as good users, regularly getting good reviews that they were quick payers.

Tracey was diagnosed with breast cancer in 2012, and died within the year. Their adult children rallied around John for the first eighteen months after Tracey's death, and then everyone seemed to get on with their lives. John tried to seem like life was continuing.

John started to dedicate more time to die-cast models. He went to trade shows and joined a club, and did research, and built up his collection. He continued to buy mainly via eBay. It was still the same family account that Tracey had set up. John had access to her emails, and the eBay account was linked to a credit card that was linked to their joint bank account. Tracey had also set up a Paypal account that was also linked to their eBay account and back to their joint bank account.

Still using the account like nothing had changed, John was looking through his purchase history one day when he noticed a small order of a bag of beads. Strange. It was $4.35 including postage or a bag of 100 yellow beads that a girl might use to make hand-made jewellery. The transaction had gone through 4 days prior. John decided to think nothing of it.

The following day, John's EFTPOS card was declined at the service station. He put the petrol on his credit card instead. He thought there must have been something wrong with the service station's terminal rather than his account.

When he arrived home, after he had prepared and eaten his dinner, he had his laptop on his lap in front of the TV. He checked eBay. There had been multiple purchases of laptops, flat screen TVs, and other consumables. As he scrolled through the purchases with horror, he realised they had all been made via the link to his joint bank account with Tracey. Her eBay account was being used by someone else.

He systematically went through each purchase and disputed the transaction. He contacted eBay by their online form, and knew he would have to wait until the following day before anyone would even look into it. Thankfully he had nothing left in his bank account. He would also have to contact the bank the following day.

When he got a fairly standard response from eBay the following day, he followed up by phone. It was a long process of being on hold and then finding someone who would listen to his explanation. He was told the account was not in his name, so the account holder would need to authorise him on the account before they would give him any information or take his query.

He spent weeks with the bank putting in claim forms to recover the money through their insurance. He spent weeks pretending to be Tracey via email to eBay to sort the account out from their end, without being able to speak with them to get it done any quicker. After months of sorting it out, John finally went through the process of shutting down Tracey's eBay account by notifying them of her death. He would begin his own account so he had proper control over it, but he lost all their purchase history and good ratings in the process.

Legal

For anyone using eBay.com.au, they must sign up for an account to use eBay services. Such an agreement is governed by the laws of New South Wales, and all notices sent to eBay should be sent to to eBay International A.G., c/- Norton Rose Fulbright, Level 18, 225 George Street, Sydney NSW 2000, or by Fax: (02) 9330 8111. eBay International AG is actually located at Helvetiastrasse 15/17, 3005 Bern, Switzerland but the Australian address is the registered agent for agreements under the laws of New South Wales.

The eBay User Agreement can be found: http://pages.ebay.com.au/help/policies/user-agreement.html?rt=nc. The User Agreement states that you will not transfer your account, but is silent as to whether an eBay store can be transferred from one account to another.

A user can close their account at any time. After doing so, eBay will retain certain customer information in accordance with their Privacy Policy. The same email address cannot be used to open another eBay account, and the eBay user ID cannot be used again. The feedback profile is taken down and cannot be seen by other eBay users.

When closing an account, eBay suggests making a one time payment for any outstanding fees, or requesting a refund for any money in the eBay account so that the balance is zero. These requests can all be made through the eBay website via their various links.

To close the account of a deceased eBay user, the site encourages the family member to contact Customer Services via the website. There is no specific policy and the death of a user is not mentioned in the User Agreement.

Practical

It would be very rare for John's situation to occur, so if an eBay account is used like a family account, then the surviving family member should change the main email address to their own, and change credit card and account details. This is contrary to the User Agreement, but a practical solution to continue using the account. Otherwise, the account should be closed and a new account created, and the consequences of this include the loss of all the credibility built up on the old account.

8 FLICKR

Joanne was a successful beauty therapist. She specialised in make-up, particularly weddings and formal events, but also stage make-up and fashion shows. She was also an amateur photographer, as she had a good eye for the artistic.

Her business exploded after she had been posting photos of her work onto Flickr. People would find her work and contact her through Flickr to come and do their make-up for their events. She began to do a lot of make up for fashion shoots, both for catwalk and magazines, as well as larger and larger stage productions.

The photos she was posting were very edgy, and she didn't take traditional portraits of her work. She posted candid shots, as well as extreme close ups and strange angles. The recognition for her work continued to grow, as did the demand for her skills.

Until she died in a car accident. She was single and in her early thirties. She had not made a Will.

Her parents struggled through with her physical and traditional assets as best they could. They cleaned out her rented apartment, and her father was able to check her emails on her laptop, because they arrived automatically into her inbox. There were lots of requests for her work. Her father was too depressed to respond to them all, to tell them she had died. He left it for a couple of weeks.

When he next checked her email, there was lots of emails, and some starting to get angry and demanding at her lack of response. There had been negative comments posted on her account on Flickr.

Joanne's father tried to log into Flickr to request that the account be closed down. But her password needed to be entered to verify her identity, and he didn't know the password. He tried contacting Flickr through an online form on their website. The following day they requested proof that Joanne had died, and proof that he had the authority to close her account. The death certificate hadn't arrived yet, so Joanne's father scanned in the booklet that had been prepared by the funeral home. There was no Will, so he asked them what they needed from him. They said they wanted ID and a copy of a court grant. Joanne's father knew this would be weeks away from being possible.

He fought with Flickr via email for a few days, sending various identification documents, along with Joanne's birth certificate which clearly identified him as her father. They finally agreed to suspend the account until he could provide the court order.

Legal

Flickr is a cloud service where photos can be uploaded, stored and shared. A user gets 1,000GB of free space when they sign up for a Flickr account through the Yahoo7 Terms of Service, since Flickr is a Yahoo company.

The laws of New South Wales applies to the Flickr Terms of Service, and the jurisdiction of the courts in New South Wales is exclusive. Notices in relation to copyright and intellectual property notices can be sent to Copyright Agent, Yahoo!7 Pty Limited, PO Box R1469, ROYAL EXCHANGE NSW 1225, Australia and one could assume that this is the address for service for all legal claims. There is also an online form for the submission of legal notices, but one has to have a Yahoo7 account for this.

There is no right of survivorship under the Yahoo7 Terms of Service, and the account is completely non-transferable. The user agrees that any rights they have to their Yahoo7 ID or contents within the account terminate upon death. Upon receipt of a copy of a death certificate, the account may be terminated and all contents therein permanently deleted. There is no means, unlike some other services, whereby an archive of the content in Flickr can be downloaded. A user can download one file at a time, but this does not help a family member trying to recover a complete digital album.

Flickr also deletes an account after two or three years of inactivity, so trying to inadvertently memorialise the account won't work either.

Practical

Because the account is non-transferrable, it is not recommended to use Flickr as a business account, as Joanne did. It is also recommended not to post directly to Flickr without storing photos someone else as well, since uploads cannot be retrieved. Family members have little options but to either leave the account alone, or close it down completely. It will be interesting if Flickr revise their stance in particular circumstances when families put their case forward.

9 PAYPAL

Michael was married to his wife Angela, and they had two children in primary school. Michael worked long hours, so when he shopped for gifts or gadgets for himself, he shopped online. He opened a Paypal account when they were only fairly new, and as the years went by, he enjoyed that more and more online retailers were allowing payment by Paypal. It was very convenient.

He had his credit card and savings account both linked to Paypal, and when he bought something, he would select which account Paypal would draw the money from. His Paypal account was also linked to the eBay account that Angela had created, and they both used eBay to buy regularly.

Overworked as he was, Michael died of a sudden heart attack.

When Angela was strong enough to start dealing with his estate, she was going through the process of closing the bank accounts in his sole name. The bank wouldn't just transfer the accounts into her name - they had to close the accounts and transfer the funds to her. This made her think of the Paypal account, which was linked to an account she had now closed.

Angela contacted Paypal, but she was not an authorised account user. So instead she had to go through the process of submitting all the proof of death documents and her identification to close the Paypal account.

This was inconvenient and time consuming, and she wondered how someone with less tenacity and online ability would cope. She had to open her own Paypal account to link to eBay, and link to her own bank accounts and credit cards, which took some time to verify everything.

Legal

The terms and conditions for a user signing up for a PayPal account in Australia can be found   here: https://www.paypal.com/au/webapps/mpp/ua/useragreement-full. The terms and conditions are exclusive to Australian users, and they adopt the warranties under the Australian Securities and Investments Commission Act 2001 or Competition and Consumer Act 2010. The User Agreement incorporates a Financial Services Guide and Product Disclosure Statement. PayPal is also a member of the Financial Services Ombudsman, so complaints can be forwarded to them.

The rights of a user under the Agreement formed when a user signs up for an account can be transferred or assigned with the prior written consent of PayPal.

An account can also be closed at any time. If the account has a negative balance, this will need to be rectified before closure. If the account has a positive balance, this will be transferred to the nominated account, or sent out by cheque. An account can also be closed if it is inactive for 3 years or more.

PayPal can be contacted at PayPal Australia, Locked Bag 10, Australia Square PO, Sydney NSW 1215 or on 1800 073 263 or 02 8223 9500.

To close a PayPal account on death is similar to an ordinary bank account. A copy of the death certificate, Will, and ID of the executor needs to be sent to PayPal. The information will be reviewed and if approved, the account will be closed.

Practical

A Paypal account cannot be a joint account. Only the main user who can authorise secondary users, but these secondary users never have any ownership of the account. Therefore, practically, PayPal should be treated like any other bank account in the sole name of the deceased. The same process applies to closing a PayPal account as it does to a bank account - providing relevant details and then signing the required forms. Any balance, if not transferred into another nominated account, should be paid by way of cheque to the estate of the deceased.

10 DROPBOX

Megan was a small business owner - she ran a florist and gift shop. She had also expanded online to sell her gifts via her website and through Facebook. She had had her laptop crash on her in the last two years, so didn't trust storing anything on a hard drive anymore. She had a business account with Dropbox.

Megan was also heavily involved in the community. She was on the committee for her netball team, and she was the secretary of the kindergarten where her niece went. Megan didn't have children of her own, but she was planning them with her fiancé.

All Megan's photos automatically uploaded to a camera folder in Dropbox. She had created a shared folder in Dropbox for all the netball team files to be stored in one place. She had also created a shared folder for the kindergarten committee, as well as a folder for the parents where information for parents was regularly uploaded.

Megan also used Dropbox to store all her business and personal files.

She hadn't thought to tell anyone how she had everything organised, because nothing was supposed to happen to her. But she was driving home one night from a netball meeting. It was dark and wet, and she swerved to avoid a possum on the road, driving straight into a tree. She died in the ambulance on the way to the hospital.

Her one staff member fumbled on to keep the business open. No one wanted the business to fail, so that the family could sell it to recover something for Megan's estate. Her employee didn't have access to Dropbox, but it wasn't crucial for day-to-day operations. At the end of the first month, it did become crucial when they had to reconcile bank accounts and prepare a Business Activity Statement. Megan's fiancé was savvy enough to find the Dropbox folder, and realise how much information was in it. He couldn't log into the online application, but she had downloaded the application onto her laptop, so they all had access to the synchronised folders still.

After some time and research, Megan's fiancé realised that the ownership of the shared folders of the netball committee and the kindergarten should be transferred to someone else, as they were not Megan's property and shouldn't be deleted or frozen. He couldn't log into Dropbox online, though, to be able to change the folder ownerships.

It took a while after contacting Dropbox directly for them to realise what he needed to achieve. He didn't want to shut down the account and just have all the files sent to him. Some of the folders should be transferred to other ownerships. It took many emails and scanned documents before Megan's fiancé was able to transfer the netball committee folder to someone else, and likewise with the kindergarten folders.

All the other documents and files were loaded onto a USB and sent to Megan's fiancé in the mail.

Legal

Opening a Dropbox account allows the user to have a personal cloud drive established for the storage of files. Certain folders can be shared. A user signing up for an account who resides outside of the United States of America, Canada and Mexico ("North America") entering into an agreement with Dropbox Ireland. The Terms of Service are governed by the Californian jurisdiction.

Dropbox hosts the user's files and content, and the ownership remains with the user. But a user may not assign any of their rights under the Terms of Service, and any such attempt will void the account.

An account can be terminated by the user at any time. Dropbox can terminate an account if it has been inactive for a consecutive 12 months.

Legal enquiries can be directed to legal@dropbox.com or to Dropbox Inc.,185

Berry Street, Suite 400, San Francisco, CA 94107. In their Help Centre, Dropbox states that a person's privacy is their number one concern, so for a loved one to access the account of a deceased person, Dropbox wants to be sure they have passed and the loved one has authority to access the files. The ask for details of the deceased, ID of the person seeking the information, and a court order. It is suggested that a copy of the Will and a copy of the grant of probate would be sufficient for "a court order".

Practical

Usually the easiest approach is to look in the Dropbox folder on the person's computers if you're authorised to do so. Many Dropbox users have all of the files from their account available in this folder, which syncs to their account online. If you don't have access to any of the person's synced computers, you might be able to access the files in the account by sending in a request to Dropbox. Once you have access, copy all the files onto another drive for ongoing access.

11 LINKEDIN

Wally Wallace, a radio shock jock on Queensland breakfast radio died after an overdose of prescription medication and alcohol. He was twice divorced with two adult children to his first wife, and a young daughter to his second. His current girlfriend didn't live with him, and seemed to bounce back from his death with a new boyfriend pretty quickly.

Wally had a Facebook page, Twitter account and LinkedIn account that were all part of his profile as a radio host for the breakfast show. His posts to Facebook were mainly done by one of the junior producers, as were most of his Twitter posts.

Occasionally he would use Twitter himself, and his posts would be highly screened by producers, with some of his posts taken down almost straight away for the protection of the station.

Wally's LinkedIn account was different. It was really just a resume-style page of his accomplishments, and was linked to celebrities and other people in the radio industry. He hadn't posted anything on LinkedIn publicly, and just kept in contact with colleagues and their careers through the platform.

Wally's second wife and his accountant were the executors under his Will, mainly benefitting his minor daughter. The executors had an argument about the online accounts and who should own them. Because of the commercial aspect of the Facebook and Twitter accounts, the executors agreed that the radio station could retain ownership of these accounts. They were turned into memorial accounts with the radio station being the owner and moderator of content that was posted.

The executors didn't want to concede on

the LinkedIn account, though. There were greater privacy issues for the people he was connected with via his LinkedIn account, and he had treated it as much more of a personal account than the others which were very focused on the fans of the breakfast show.

It turned out that it was a fight not worth fighting, since the LinkedIn account did not survive Wally's death. It was deleted by LinkedIn.

Legal

By signing up for a LinkedIn account, the user agrees to the terms in the User Agreement which can be found here: https://www.linkedin.com/legal/user-agreement. If the user resides outside of the United States, the agreement is with LinkedIn Ireland. Any user submits to the jurisdiction of California USA.

Terms in the User Agreement require the user to keep their username and password secure and confidential, and does not allow any part of the account to be transferred.

Any content or information a user posts

onto LinkedIn remains the ownership of that user, but the user grants a licence to LinkedIn to copy, modify, distribute and publish the information. To end this licence, the user needs to delete the content or information, or close their account. An account can be terminated by the user at any time.

LinkedIn can be contacted at LinkedIn Ireland, Attn: Agreement Matters (Legal), Wilton Plaza, Wilton Place, Dublin 2 Ireland or via their Help Centre online.

LinkedIn provide an online form to notify them of a deceased account holder, and begin the process of removing their account: https://help.linkedin.com/app/ask/path/ts-rdmlp. They want a proof of death, such as a death certificate or a link to an obituary up front, and will ask for additional information that they require. No further information is provided about what can be removed, if anything, from the account before it is deleted.

Practical

Practically, it is unlikely that a LinkedIn account has much value, except perhaps in the connections. If this is the case, and a business partner wants the same connections, then they should go through the list of connections of the deceased user and make those connections themselves. It is unlikely that any posted content can be recovered, but it will not be deleted either, so if there are articles written by the deceased that a family member wants to keep, then a copy should just be made of the content of the article. LinkedIn accounts should then be deleted so that the account of a deceased is not always trying to find new connections.

12 PINTEREST

Monica became passionate about scrapbooking after her children left home. She began by scrapbooking all the old photos of her children, and her obsession grew from there. She initially couldn't find quality products or stencils that she wanted to use, so she began sourcing materials overseas, and then even commissioning stencils to be made by a Chinese company.

She soon saw that other scrap-bookers were having the same trouble as her, at finding good quality material at a reasonable price (as soon as scrapbooking was mentioned, prices seemed to be marked up!) in Australia. So she began buying more than she needed when she bought something for herself, and she would sell the rest on eBay.

Quite quickly, she formed a strong following on eBay and her materials were snapped up quickly, as she sold them for a fixed price and kept the prices cheap. Her orders of materials grew, as did her sales, until before she knew it, she had a business.

Monica also opened a Pinterest account when she started selling on eBay. She would post a picture of every page she scrapbooked. She would post pictures of the methods she used, the stencils she used, and sometimes step-by-step pictures of how to achieve a similar effect. Her Pinterest account followers grew exponentially.

Monica was killed in a car accident when a truck ran a red light, trying to get through before it changed, and Monica had already started into the intersection when her light turned green. Her death was instant.

As well as all the grief her family were dealing with, they soon learnt that Monica had not formalised her business, even though she was earning over $60,000 per year making her scrapbooking sales. The value of her business essentially ended up being the stock and equipment that she had stored at home, which was not much, instead of a business that could be sold.

Her son saw the goodwill potential in Monica's Pinterest account and approached a number of similar small business owners to see if they would purchase Monica's Pinterest account from them for the value in the follower base. Even though they did end up finding a business that was very interested in purchasing Monica's list of followers on Pinterest, Monica's son soon discovered that Monica's account was just a personal account, and Pinterest wanted to terminate the account. If it were a business account, the ownership could have been transferred.

After months of arguing, and losing the value in the Pinterest account due to the passage of time, and also losing the potential purchaser of the Pinterest account, Monica's son finally convinced Pinterest that they could treat Monica's account like a business account and agreed to a transfer. By the time they agreed, there was no point.

Legal

By signing up for a Pinterest account, a user agrees to be bound by the Terms of Service and Privacy Policy which can be found here: https://about.pinterest.com/en/terms-service.

Pinterest grants the user a non-transferrable licence to use their products within the Acceptable Usage Policy. Any content that is posted by a user remains the property of the user, but the user grants Pinterest with a worldwide licence to use, reproduce, modify, store and publish that content. Other users can store or share your content, which remains even after deactivation of the user account.

The laws governing the Terms of Service are those of the State of California, and the parties to the agreement submit to the jurisdiction of the state courts in San Francisco County.

The Terms of Service do not address the death or incapacity of a user, but a quick search in the Help area produced information that Pinterest will deactivate an account of a deceased user if the family gets in contact with them via care@pinterest.com. They need the full details of the person who has passed, documentation verifying the family relationship, and a copy of the death certificate.

Practical

Practically, in Monica's situation, there does not appear to have been any solution for her Pinterest account. Her account should be deactivated after her death, and does not have any value in transferring it as an asset. There is no information about whether the uploaded material can be downloaded or retrieved by the family before the account is closed.

13 SKYPE

Trevor was a serving member with the Royal Australia Army. He was regularly away from his wife Fiona and their young children. When he was away, they relied on Skype to communicate every night. The ability to be able to have video calls kept the children in better contact with their dad, and Trevor and Fiona got more benefit out of it than audio only calls.

When Trevor was deployed to the Middle East, he was able to use Skype most days to call home, so that it didn't feel like he was as far away from home for Fiona and the children. He returned home safely from his deployment, but had been able to keep up with the children's development and see them regularly for the months that he was away.

Trevor died in an accident that wasn't work related, after he had returned home.

When Fiona was ready, she began the process of dealing with all of Trevor's online accounts. Skype was one of the hardest. The account could be terminated, as in recurring payments ceased and software no longer used. However, the account could not be deleted completely.

Fiona had to remove as much personal information about Trevor from his account as she could, but the user account could never be deleted. She removed his profile picture and put in false information into the account, so that no one could identify who owned the account. But the Skype Name was his full name, and that would remain forever. She was assured that Skype would eventually tag the account as inactive, and it would be removed from search results when that happened.

But a few months down the track, distressingly Fiona received a Skype call from Trevor's account! It was like a prank call, as the person hung up immediately, but then the messages started from Trevor's account. Some sicko had hacked into Trevor's account and was using it to torment his family.

Fiona reported it to Skype, and removed Trevor from the contacts in her own Skype account. But the problem wasn't resolved quickly, and Fiona continued to receive link up and message requests from the hacker.

The initial shock of receiving the call from Trevor was the worst, but once Fiona got over that, she was just angry with the hacker and with Skype for allowing this to happen.

Legal

Skype has been bought by Microsoft, so the same Terms of Use apply as for Hotmail and Outlook services. The Skype Help page only provides some basic information on how to cancel a subscription account: <u>https://support.skype.com/en/faq/FA1881/</u> <u>how-do-i-cancel-my-subscription#1</u>.
Presumably the same Next of Kin Policy would also apply to Skype as to all Microsoft services. Originally, before Microsoft bought Skype, a Skype account could not be deleted -

only personal information could be removed but the username and account history remained indefinitely.

Practical

It is likely that the Skype account can now be completely removed on notification of death, like other Microsoft accounts. Microsoft would keep some basic information, and would not allow the same account name to be used again, but this should remove any hacking problems that Fiona faced. The deletion of the account will not be quick - proof documents will still need to be provided and a process followed until the account would be deleted.

14 INSTAGRAM

Charles was a wine critic. It came about just because he was a fan of wine, not because he worked in the industry. He began posting a star rating for wines that he tried on his Twitter account, and began posting shots of wine bottles, glasses of wine and other trendy wine photos on his Instagram account.

After doing this for a few years, and establishing quite a following, he began getting sent bottles of wine for free, for review. This then lead to him being offered a regularly fortnightly short column in a popular weekend newspaper. So as well as getting lots of free wine, he was now also earning a little bit of money from it, and enjoying the whole thing immensely, since his weekends revolved around trips to wineries for "research".

Charles continued to drive traffic to his Instagram account from his fortnightly newspaper column, and his photos were often shared broadly, perpetuating the cycle and causing more followers.

Never having robust lungs, Charles contracted pneumonia one year, and also a secondary infection. Antibiotics seemed to work initially, but then they stopped working and Charles declined and died within two weeks.

The newspaper wanted to buy Charles' photos off the family, both by way of some financial support, but also so they could use some of his older reviews to continue the column for a while with someone else writing it instead.

Luckily, Charles' passwords were all saved into his laptop, so his family could log into his accounts as if they were him. Charles' family worked out that they could use Instaport to export all of Charles' Instagram photos from his account and download them onto another drive. All his photos could then be sold to the newspaper.

If they couldn't log into his account directly and use Instaport, his family don't believe that Instagram would have given them a downloaded or archived copy of his account, and all his photos would have been lost. But now having no further need for the Instagram account, his family then contacted Instagram by email and had the account shut down.

Legal

The Terms of Use for an Instagram account that a user agrees to when using the service can be found here: https://help.instagram.com/47874555885251 1. A user agrees not to transfer any rights, and to keep their passwords secret and secure.

A user can terminate their account at any time, but they need to do so from within the account; so signed in rather than through a request in the Help section. None of the data (photos, comments, or personal connections) can be accessed through the account after the account is terminated, though those materials and data may persist in the Instagram service itself for others to access. It appears that the licence a user gives to Instagram to use and republish their content does not cease on termination of the account.

Users agree that the governing law for the agreement are the laws of the State of California, and the Terms of Use specifically exclude United Nations conventions.

Instagram has a policy in relation to an account of a deceased person: they will memorialise an account on receipt of proof of death from anyone, but they will only remove an account at the request of an immediate family member. The immediate family member also needs to provide proof of authority as legal personal representative under the local law.

A memorialised account cannot be logged into by anyone else, and cannot be altered. The content is only visible to the audience that the user already had, and not to the public. People can post to the deceased person's account.

To report the death, the links can be found by searching in the Help section of Instagram, and then filling in the form to report a person has deceased: https://help.instagram.com/contact/452224988254813.

Practical

The best practical advice so far, even if it is contrary to most user agreements, is to have access to the deceased's account; either by way of them leaving a list of usernames and passwords, or by an automatically remembered password on their device. There was no information about whether Instagram would help download the content of the deceased's account for the family after death, so it would be preferable to log in as the deceased to download the content via Instaport as Charles' family did.

15 KINDLE/AMAZON

Margaret, a 58 year old woman, received a Kindle device a few years prior as a birthday gift. It had become her prize possession. Already an avid reader, she took a little while to get over not holding onto a physical book anymore, but once she embraced the Kindle she couldn't believe she used to carry around piles of books. Her husband Kevin would just shake his head at her, but it was him who made sure she picked it up and didn't leave it behind in a cafe when she put it down.

She was spending about $40 per month on Amazon, buying books for her Kindle. So after three years, she had spent about $1,500 and had accumulated a lot of books. Her taste was varied, but there were a lot of classics and award winning fiction that she really wanted her family to read. She kept a Good Reads account and made recommendations to her friends and family, and posted her ratings of each book and updates on where she was up to.

When Margaret was diagnosed with advanced cervical cancer she read her Kindle during treatment, and had it with her in hospital all the way to the end. On her deathbed, she called her eldest granddaughter over to her. Her granddaughter was 9 years old and also developing a love for reading. Margaret gave her granddaughter her Kindle, amongst a lot of tears from her, her daughter and her granddaughter. Two days later she was dead.

Margaret's daughter, Kylie, was the mother of Alice, the granddaughter who was given the Kindle. Margaret's husband cancelled the recurring $40 per month from their credit card for the Amazon account. Kylie tried to log into Margaret's Amazon account to add her own credit card to continue the account, but she couldn't work out Margaret's password and couldn't recover the lost password because it was password protected.

Kylie then looked into adding a new account to the Kindle, but it would have wiped all Margaret's books off Alice's Kindle, and Kylie knew there were books on there that Margaret would have wanted Alice to read. If the Amazon account was deleted, all the books Margaret had bought would be gone as the books are only licensed for her to use and she doesn't own them.

So there was nothing to be done. The Amazon account couldn't be deleted, because they wanted to keep the books, and couldn't be used because they couldn't add a new payment method. Alice's Kindle could be used to read any of the books that Margaret had bought, but it was now a static device because nothing else could be added to it, and Alice couldn't download anything she wanted on it.

Legal

In Australia, those who sign up to an Amazon account gets a limited access to Amazon Services through Amazon Australia Services Inc. Part of Amazon Services includes the free

Kindle App, and ebooks bought from Amazon and delivered to the Kindle App or device. Many Amazon products are not available to Australian users, as Amazon will not ship most of their products internationally. The Conditions of Use can be found here: http://www.amazon.com.au/gp/help/custo mer/display.html?nodeId=201374360.

The Conditions of Use grants the user a limited non-exclusive, non-transferable, non-sublicensable license to access and make personal and non-commercial use of the Amazon Services. The user is responsible of maintaining the confidentially of their account and password *and* restricting access to the user's computer, in case someone can log in easily by a password automatically saved in the browser.

Disputes in Australia are directed to Amazon.com's registered agent: Corporation Service Company, 300 Deschutes Way SW, Suite 304, Tumwater, WA 98501. But all disputes must be first arbitrated by the American Arbitration Association (AAA) under its rules. Users submit to the jurisdiction of the laws of the state of

Washington, USA.

For ebooks bought from Amazon and delivered to your Kindle device or Kindle app, you are granted a non-exclusive right to view, use, and display such Kindle content an unlimited number of times, solely on the Kindle or a Kindle reading application. The Kindle content is licensed, not sold, to you. You may not sell, rent, lease, distribute, broadcast, sublicense, or otherwise assign any rights to the Kindle content or any portion of it to any third party.

The Terms of Use for Amazon, and the Help section for Amazon do not address the death of a user. The forums for Amazon users address it at length, but only with speculation about breaching Terms of Use by passing on the device with the account and password details.

Practical

This is a very similar situation from an iTunes account, but at least with iTunes the content can be burned onto other devices. With Kindle books, they are on one device or application linked to the account. There is nothing that can be done about this practically. The deceased's family will need a dedicated device for the downloads from the account, but the downloads cannot be transferred, and if the account is changed on the device then all previous downloads are lost.

16 YOUTUBE

Cruz was wild and crazy. He attracted similar high-energy people to him, and he liked to push his physical boundaries with extreme sports. He rode moto-X, rode a road motorbike, skydived, base jumped, wakeboarded, snowboarded, and did anything that caused his body to go fast and his mind to peak on adrenalin.

As one of the early adopters of the GoPro cameras, mounts and accessories, Cruz was dedicated to catching all the adventures that he and his mates got up to. He avidly edited, added music and uploaded clips onto YouTube. He gained a massive following over the years, and also picked up sponsorship deals and did fairly well on the moto-X circuit. He made money videoing other people's experiences and selling them their footage, such as tandem skydive jumps, and also instructing snowboarding during the snow season.

His parents had always said it was bound to happen one day, and it did - Cruz was killed. But he was killed on his road motorbike by a car coming around a blind corner on the wrong side of the road. It wasn't a particularly risky activity he was doing, and it wasn't an error that Cruz made - it was just an accident.

Cruz had a lot of un-edited footage, and hours and hours of video uploaded onto YouTube. His family decided that they could make at least one DVD out of his footage, and they could sell it and create a foundation in his name to help people with spinal injuries to experience extreme sports again.

YouTube is owned by Google, but Cruz had not appointed an Inactive Account Manager to take over should something happen to him. So it was not an easy process for his family to contact Google and provide the death certificate and other identification documentation to get his account switched over. There was some argument that Google was only going to allow limited access, which would not have allowed for downloading the videos from YouTube, but with the passage of time and provision of the correct information, Google was eventually convinced.

Cruz's sister was a black sheep in the family, and had a personality disorder. She objected to the whole idea of creating a foundation and a DVD to raise money. She objected to everything all the time. She threatened to take court action to stop the family getting access to Cruz's YouTube videos. Luckily they were only threats, and Google didn't get wind of her objections. If Google had thought there was any doubt in who they were giving access to the account, the whole thing would have either been over or delayed significantly.

Legal

YouTube is owned by Google, so refer to the details above Google in Chapter 3 above.

Practical

Reiterating Chapter 3 above, everyone with a Google account should implement the Inactive Account Manager feature. But if someone has passed away without having done so, it would be prudent for the executor or family member to try logging into the Google account on the deceased person's device. If the account can be accessed, then download all the content. Accessing someone else's account without their permission (because they have died) is not ideal and could even be in breach of the terms of service of the Google account, but practically this is often the quickest and easiest way to get access. If the family do not have the password and cannot otherwise access the account, they would need to contact Google to get access and this may or may not be granted.

17 EVERNOTE

Adam was a writer. Since he discovered Evernote, it has been the hub spot of all his writing, and more. He makes notes for himself, he makes to-do lists, he saves his research to Evernote, he collates his book outlines, and he quickly writes a good paragraph or two into a note when it comes to him. He has used Evernote during his last five novels, and he has also written a non-fiction book.

Adam dies suddenly, and accidentally, from a cocktail of prescription drugs and alcohol that he was taking to try to increase his performance.

He was single and his family didn't really know how he worked. He had the Evernote software on his desktop, so when he family were going through his things, they found all the notes and research, and another partially written book. There was also notes and research on other future projects. Evernote also contained the notes and research from his last six books, with drafts and extra ideas. All the content was potentially valuable.

Unfortunately, Adam hadn't written a Will appointing anyone as his executor. Evernote is one of the online software companies that recognise executors in Wills easily, and can release account information and content to a nominated executor.

Because Adam didn't have a Will, Evernote is careful about privacy, and wouldn't release account information or content to next of kin. Adam's estate was substantial enough that his family had to apply for Letters of Administration to administer his intestate estate. When they had obtained this grant, they were able to forward a copy onto Evernote, which recognised it and were then able to release account information to the administrators.

Legal

Evernote consists of the Evernote software, and other products or services that can be bought through the Evernote Marketplace. Users agree to be party to an agreement incorporating the Terms of Service which can be found here: https://evernote.com/legal/tos.php. If you reside outside of the United States, Canada and Brasil, then the other party to this contract is Evernote GmbH, a company headquartered in Zurich, Switzerland (Walchestrasse 9, 8006 Zurich, Switzerland).

You are granted a personal non-assignable and non-exclusive license to use Evernote. You retain copyright and all other rights to the content you submit, post or display on Evernote, subject to granting Evernote a licence so that the content and data can be made accessible through Evernote.

You may deactivate your account at any time. There are a number of different levels that can be achieved. You can cancel a subscription account and return to a free account. You can download an archive of your entire content before you delete the content on Evernote and then ask for the account to be deactivated. If you ask for the account to be deactivated, Evernote will not delete your content, so you can reactivate the account. It is optional to completely remove your email and username when you deactivate your account, in which case you would never be able to reactivate it.

For Australian users, the agreement is governed in all respects by the laws of Switzerland and shall be considered to have been made and accepted in Switzerland, without regard to conflict of law provisions.

Evernote has a specific provision in its Terms of Service entitled "What Happens To My Account When I Die?". It states that Evernote will do its utmost to preserve your privacy and will not provide account information or content to anyone, even next of kin, unless they are legally obligated to do so. Evernote encourages users to include account information and instructions in your Will or estate plan.

Legal notices can be sent to Evernote GmbH, Walchestrasse 9, 8006 Zurich,

Switzerland.

Practical

Once your executor has access to your Account Information, they should cancel any subscription that you have. A subscription ends from the end of the then-current billing period. If you only have a free account, there are no subscriptions to cancel.

Your executor can then export all your notes and content as a html file or xml file - you can get instructions from Evernote directly on how to do this. Once all the content has been exported, make sure you delete all the notes and content from Evernote.

Then deactivate the account by logging into the Evernote website and click the "Deactivate Account" link in the account settings.

If you want to completely remove the email address and username after the account is deactivated, you can contact Evernote Support by email to let them know the account is deactivated and you want the email address and username removed from Evernote's system.

18 DOMAINS AND WEBSITE HOSTS

Sam was a small business owner who had a number of small businesses, some online, and one offline. She had embraced online marketing, and had registered 30 domains, and had a number of different hosting accounts, and numerous websites, sub-domains and sales funnels.

In some cases, the same company with whom she registered her domain name also provided the hosting. A couple of her websites were with Wix, however, and others were Wordpress websites. She also used Lead Pages and Click Funnels for sales pages, and these used sub-domains which she had filtered through Cloud Flare.

Her online arrangements were quite complex, and her husband and family had no understanding of her setup. If she had left detailed instructions, it may have been worked out within a few months.

As it was, her husband became aware of domain names over the next two years, as they came up for renewal. The domain name registrar would email and say that the domain was due for renewal, and he would then know which registrar they were registered with. Some domains were not bothered to be renewed, and others lay dormant until he found out about them.

Her main offline business was sold, and the domain name and website hosting needed to be transferred to the new owner. Sam's husband contacted auDA (.au Domain Administration Ltd) and found out the password for the domain and with whom it was registered. He could then use the grant of probate he obtained, and submit this along with the transfer documents to transfer the domain to the new business owner. This took him a while to figure out, and settlement of the business was held up until he had achieved it.

Luckily, the offline business website was also hosted with the domain, so when the domain was transferred, the registrar asked if the hosting was to be transferred too, and Sam's husband was able to do this easily. If it wasn't, often a website has a link at the very bottom saying who created it which could be an indication as to where it is hosted (for example, Wix sites). However, if it was a Word Press website, this is not the case.

Legal

A domain name is registered to a registrant by the domain name registrar (the entity responsible for the provision of domain name licences). .au Domain Administration Limited is the domain registrar for all websites ending in .au. Any entity wanting to register an .au website must have an ABN.

A registrant can transfer the ownership of a domain from one registrant to another by completing a Domain Transfer of Ownership form, either with the domain registrar directly, or through a third party retailer. On the death of the owner, the domain name automatically becomes part of the deceased estate, and can be dealt with by the executor contacting the domain name registrar[1].

The accounts that registrants usually hold to buy domain names are with a third party retailer, that often offers other services, including website hosting. These accounts cannot usually be transferred as they are just licensed accounts under a terms of service agreement. When transferring the domain name, the beneficiary will need to have their own retailer account set up so that the domain name registrar can transfer the domain name. Similarly, where a website is hosted, the content and programming of the website can be transferred to a new host in the name of the beneficiary.

Practical

Domain names are often the most valuable digital assets that can be held and transferred easily. If the deceased has not left details

---

[1] 'Complaints (Registrant Eligibility) Policy' 2004-1, .au Domain Administration Ltd <http://www.auda.org.au/policies/2004-01/> at 6 November 2015.

about where the domain names are registered, then you can contact the .au Domain Administration Limited, or like Sam's husband, you can wait until renewal emails are sent out every year or two. There is a formal process to transfer domain names, similar to transferring real estate (not quite as complicated), which can be followed by the executor of the estate once they have Probate or Letters of Administration.

It is important to note that there are numerous domain name registrars, and only some are able to process .au websites. Only people with an ABN can own a .au website. But there are many more website hosts than there are domain registrars. So if you do not leave a comprehensive explanation of what you own, then things can get lost.

19 GENERAL REVIEW OF LAWS OF ESTATE ASSETS

What an estate asset is

Before we can determine what a digital asset is and how a digital asset should be managed as part of a deceased estate, we should review what a general asset is. In Victoria, the property that can be disposed of by will is defined in s4 of the *Wills Act 1997* (Vic):

> 4(1) A person may, by will, dispose of -
> a) any property to which the person is entitled at the time of his or her death, whether or not the

entitlement of the person did or did not exist at the date of the making of the will; and

b) any property to which the personal representative of that person becomes entitled, by virtue of the office of personal representative to that person, after the death of that person -

other than property of which the testator is trustee.

4(2) In this section *property* includes -

a) a contingent, executory or future interest in property -

    i) whether the person becomes entitled to the interest by way of the instrument which created the interest or otherwise; and

    ii) whether that person has or has not been ascertained as the person in whom the interest may become vested; and

b) a right of entry or recovery of property or a right to call for the transfer of title of property.

"Property" is also defined in section 5 of the *Administration and Probate Act 1958* (Vic) as including a thing in action and any interest in real or personal property. The same definition section defines ones "estate" as meaning real and personal estate. Similarly, the *Property Law Act 1958 (Vic)* defines "property" as any thing in action, and any interest in real or personal property. Real property and personal property are not specifically defined[2].

"Personal estate" was defined in s3 of the *Wills Act 1958* (Vic) and has come to be known to include:

1. leasehold estates
2. other chattels real (other than a leasehold)
3. moneys
4. shares of government and other funds
5. securities for money
6. debts
7. choses in action
8. rights
9. credits
10. goods, and
11. all other property whatsoever which by law devolves upon the executor or administrator and to any share or

---

[2] Property Law Act 1958 (Vic), s18.

interest therein.[3]

Someone's personal estate does not include jointly held assets, assets over which they have control but not absolute ownership, and superannuation. Assets that do not form part of the property or estate of a deceased cannot be disposed of by disposition in a Will[4]. However, for some of these non-estate assets, the control can be passed through the Will, such as for a sole member of a SMSF or an appointor of a family trust[5].

An outline of roles and obligations of executors in relation to estate assets

The essential role of an executor is to take control of the estate assets, call in these assets, ascertain and discharge the liabilities (as at the date of death and those incurred by virtue of the administration process) and then distribute the remaining estate assets to the

---

[3] Lexis Nexis, 'Property and elections' Wills Probate and Administration Vic,
<http://lexisnexis.com.ezproxy.collaw.edu.au/au/legal/delivery/Prin...3 A527106816%Fformatted_do&fromCart=false&jobHandle=2827%3A5 27106816>.

[4] David M Haines QC, Construction of Wills in Australia, (2007), 89.

[5] Allan Swan, 'Personal Ownership v Control', Australian Estate Planning (6-100) CCH.

beneficiaries. During the period of administration, the legal and equitable interest in the estate assets vest in the executor. Once administration has been completed, the equitable interest in the estate assets pass to the beneficiaries. It can be crucial to determine when administration finishes and the executor becomes the trustee of the estate assets for the beneficiaries, as duties and obligations can be slightly different[6].

The authority to act is derived from the will, and the deceased's assets vest in the executor from the date of death. If the deceased is intestate, the assets vest with the State Trustees Ltd pursuant to section 19 of the *Administration and Probate Act 1958* (Vic) pending the issue of the grant of letters of administration, and then the assets vest in the administrator. Section 27 of the *Administration and Probate Act*[7] places an administrator in the same position as an executor once the grant has been made[8].

---

[6] Lexis Nexis, 'Duties powers and rights of personal representatives' Wills Probate and Administration Vic,
<http://lexisnexis.com.ezproxy.collaw.edu.au/au/legal/delivery/Prin...3 A527106816%Fformatted_do&fromCart=false&jobHandle=2827%3A5 27106816>.

[7] Administration and Probate Act 1958 (Vic).

[8] Lexis Nexis, 'Control of estate assets of deceased person' Wills

Personal representatives have always had the ability at common law and in equity to administer an estate. In Victoria, the statutes that codify some of the duties, powers and rights of personal representatives are the *Administration and Probate Act*[9], the *Trustee Act*[10], and the *Property Law Act*[11]. But there are no established or fixed number of duties, powers or rights. Many are derived from the powers explicitly stated in the Will directly.[12]

Asset classification

A personal representative must ascertain what assets belong to the estate as soon as possible, and this will involve a level of classification of assets - whether they are estate assets or not, whether there is a power of control over non-estate assets, and what jurisdiction covers assets that are not Victorian[13]. A classification

---

Probate and Administration Vic,
<http://lexisnexis.com.ezproxy.collaw.edu.au/au/legal/delivery/Prin...3
A527106816%Fformatted_do&fromCart=false&jobHandle=2827%3A5
27106816>.

[9] Above, n10.

[10] Trustee Act 1958 (Vic).

[11] Property Law Act 1958 (Vic).

[12] Above, n9.

[13] Above, n9.

as to whether property is movable or immovable will determine the relevant jurisdiction[14].

For immovable property such as land and immovable tangible goods (physical or actual items), where they are situated is where they are located, and the land or item will be regulated by the law applying to the location of the property. For example company shares are located where the company is incorporated or where the shares are registered[15], and bank accounts are located at the branch where the account is kept[16]. Movable property will be regulated by the law of the domicile of the deceased at the date of his or her death[17].

Where property is not in Australia, the doctrine of renvoi can come into play, being that the law of the foreign jurisdiction where the immovable property is located may refer back to the law of the domicile of the deceased. Though the issue has not been

---

[14] Haque v Haque (No 2) (1965) 114 CLR 98.

[15] R v Williams (1942) AC 541.

[16] R v Lovitt (1912) AC 212.

[17] Certoma, GI, The Law of Succession in NSW (4th ed, 2010), 21.

settled in Australia, it appears that double renvoi is the approach that Australian courts are likely to take to the law of succession so that they would refer back to the foreign country's law[18]. This becomes relevant as many digital assets are governed by foreign jurisdictions, so if the Australian courts applied double renvoi to digital assets then the jurisdiction relevant to the foreign asset will often be found in the terms and conditions of the agreement that the account user signed with the custodian online business.

---

[18] Ibid.

20 REVIEW OF THE LAW OF DIGITAL ASSETS

Introduction to digital assets

Gone are the days of looking through old boxes of papers, filing cabinets and diaries. Files are now electronic; emails have replaced letters and hard-copy bills; novels are on ebook readers; photos, audio and video are data files; and accounts are accessible digitally with a username and password.[19] What hasn't been considered thoroughly is how these electronic files and accounts are classified -

---

[19] Beth Castell, 'Digital assets and estate planning - life and death in the digital age' (2014) 17(3) Retirement & Estate Planning Bulletin.

are they estate assets or non-estate assets over which control can be passed? Or are they a mere licence to use a service or piece of software which is extinguished on death of the party to the agreement? How much of what is self-published online about a person's own identity can be considered intellectual property, if any, and can therefore be recovered or controlled by the legal personal representative?

Digital assets could vary substantially in actual, perceived and sentimental values; from the electronic family photos stored in a cloud drive, to the electronic portfolio of professional photos of a photographer; or the collection of electronic clips and research of a family's genealogy, to the research and draft notes of a published author of their next work. WebCease presents as a fact that that average internet user has US$36,000 worth of 'unprotected' digital assets (approximately AUD$50,000) and that on average an American values their digital assets at US$55,000 (approximately AUD$78,000)[20].

---

[20] Digital Asset Facts (2014) Web Cease < http://www.webcease.com/about/digital-asset-facts> at 5 November 2015.

There may be some over-estimation of the value of some assets and under-estimation of others in these figures, but they are substantial enough for an executor of an estate to be concerned about collecting.

The ownership and conditions of access to many of these digital accounts are regulated by the terms of service entered into when the person initially signs up to them. Many of these terms of service agreements haven't even considered what happens when the primary user dies. To further complicate the situation, most online services are operated from or backed up to a another country, in another legal jurisdiction.

The common sense advice to date has been to have a list or private register of all relevant usernames and passwords for each service, along with instructions for a relative or legal personal representative to take over. However, the terms of service of many of the online service providers prohibits the sharing of passwords or the transfer of accounts to a third party, and forbid any person from accessing another person's account, even after death[21].

Review of law in Australia

There is no law specific to succession and digital assets in Australia. The laws outlined in part 2 above are those in Victoria which apply to the succession of assets generally, and the other States and Territories have a similar scheme.

There are privacy laws in Australia that could apply to the privacy of a deceased's online information after death in the *Privacy Act*[22], and this includes the amendment in the *Privacy Amendment (Enhancing Privacy Protection) Act*[23] which requires mandatory data retention for 2 years and allowing access to a person's metadata.

The *Copyright Act*[24] determines that copyright lasts for 70 years after death, which could apply to those unpublished master pieces in electronic format which could be valuable to a deceased estate.

---

[21] Dr Martin Gibbs, et al 'Digital registers and estate planning' (2013) 16(3) Retirement & Estate Planning Bulletin.

[22] Privacy Act 1988 (Cth).

[23] Privacy Amendment (Enhancing Privacy Protection) Act 2012 (Cth).

[24] Copyright Act 1958 (Cth).

The Commonwealth enacted the *Electronic Transaction Act 1999* and each state and territory enacted a similar Act which generally mirrors the Commonwealth Act. The *Electronic Transactions (Victoria) Act*[25] commenced operation on 1 September 2000 for the purposes of giving legal effect to electronic contracts and electronic signatures, to permit documents to be produced electronically, and to allow information that must be retained to be recorded and retained electronically.[26] This Act contains definitions for 'data', 'data storage device', 'electronic communication', 'information' and 'information system' which could be useful for any future legislation that could be enacted regarding the succession of digital assets.

Review of law internationally

The *Uniform Fiduciary Access to Digital Assets Act* ("UFADA Act")[27] in the United States of

---

[25] Electronic Transactions (Victoria) Act 2000 (Vic).

[26] Yee Fen Lim, Cyberspace Law, (2002), 76.

[27] Uniform Fiduciary Access to Digital Assets Act (2014) Uniform Law Commission <http://www.uniformlaws.org/shared/docs/Fiduciary%20Access%20to%20Digital%20Assets/2014_UFADAA_Final.pdf> at 28 June 2015.

America appears to be the first piece of legislation in the world dealing specifically with succession and digital assets. At the annual conference of the Uniform Law Commission in July 2014, the UFADA Act was approved and recommended for enactment in all States.

The approach of the UFADA Act is to address the rights of a fiduciary on the death or incapacity of the principal, and to facilitate access for the fiduciary to digital accounts while respecting the privacy and intent of the account holder. Under the UFADA Act a personal representative is presumed to have access to all of the principal's digital assets unless that is contrary to the principal's express intent[28]. An entity may not refuse to provide access to online records to the fiduciary any more than the entity, such as a bank, can refuse to provide the fiduciary with access to hard copy records[29].

The UFADA Act defines a digital assets as "a record that is electronic". It refers to any type of electronically-stored information such

---

[28] Ibid, 2.
[29] Ibid, 7.

as: 1) any information stored on a computer and other digital devices; 2) content uploaded onto websites, ranging from photos to documents; and 3) rights in digital property, such as domain names or digital entitlements associated with online games.[30]

The fiduciary's authority to access digital assets of the principal is confirmed when the fiduciary obtains access directly using a password of the principal, which is usually the case, or the fiduciary can also obtain access pursuant to the UFADA Act by contacting the entity. The fiduciary has the same authority as the principal account holder, and is also subject to the terms and conditions of the account[31]. Access by the fiduciary is not considered a transfer or other use that would violate the anti-transfer terms of a service agreement[32].

An example is provided on page 18 of the UFADA Act:

Example 1 - Access to digital assets by

---

[30] Ibid.

[31] Ibid, 16.

[32] Ibid, 18.

personal representative. D dies with a will that is silent with respect to digital assets. D has a bank account for which D received only electronic statements, D has stored photos in a cloud-based Internet account, and D has an email account with a company that provides electronic-communication services to the public. The personal representative of D's estate needs access to the electronic bank account statements, the photo account and the emails.

The personal representative of D's estate has the authority to access D's electronic banking statements and D's photo account, which both fall under the UFADA Act's definition of a "digital asset". This means that, if these accounts are password-protected or otherwise unavailable to the personal representative, then the bank and the photo account service must give access to the personal representative when the request is made in accordance with Section 9. If the terms of service agreement permits D to transfer the accounts electronically, then the personal representative of D's estate can use that procedure for transfer as well.

The personal representative of D's estate is also able to request that the email account service provider grant access to emails sent or received by D; the Electronic Communications Privacy Act (ECPA) permits the service provider to release the catalogue to the personal representative. The service provider also must provide the personal representative access to the content of an electronic communication sent or received by D if the service provider is permitted under 18 U.S.C. Section 2702(b) to disclose the content. The bank may release the catalogue of electronic communications or content of an electronic communication for which it is the originator or the addressee because the bank is not subject to the ECPA.[33]

The UFADA Act also deals with jurisdiction at section 8(c) by making a choice

---

[33] Ibid, 18.

of law provision in a terms of service agreement unenforceable. An example is provided on page 20 of the UFADA Act:

Example 5 - Access notwithstanding terms in a terms-of-service agreement. D, who is domiciled in state X, dies. D was a professional photographer who stored valuable digital photos in an online storage account provided by C. P is appointed by a court in state X to administer D's estate. P needs access to D's online storage account to inventory and appraise D's estate assets and to file D's estate tax return. During D's lifetime, D entered into a terms-of-service agreement with C for the online storage account. The choice-of-law provision selects the law of state Y to govern the contractual rights and duties under the terms-of-service agreement. A provision of the terms-of-service agreement prohibits fiduciary access to the digital assets of an account holder, but D did not agree to that provision by an affirmative act separate from D's assent to other provisions of the terms-of-service agreement. UFADA Act has been enacted by state X but not by state Y. Because P's access to D's assets is fundamental to carrying out P's fiduciary duties, a court should apply subsections (b) and (c) of this act under the law of state X to void the terms-of-service agreement provision prohibiting P's access to D's online account, even though the terms-of-service agreement selected the law of state Y to govern the contractual rights and duties under the terms-of-service agreement.[34]

Section 9 of the UFADA Act details how a fiduciary can request access, control, or a copy of the digital asset, and the method of compliance. An example is provided on page 24 of the UFADA Act:

Example - Fiduciary control over a digital asset. D dies with a will disposing of all D's assets to D's spouse, S. E is the personal representative for D's estate. D left a bank account, for which D only receive online statements, and a blog.

E as personal representative of D's

[34] Ibid, 20.

estate has access to both of D's accounts and can request the passwords from the custodians of both accounts. If D's agreement with the bank requires that transferring the underlying title to the account be done in person, through a hard copy signed by the account holder and the bank manager, then E must comply with those procedures and cannot transfer the funds in the account electronically. If the terms of service agreement for the blog permitted D to transfer the blog electronically, then E can make the transfer electronically as well.

Subsection (c) established 60 days as the appropriate time for compliance, so the bank and the blog custodian must provide access and/or control to E within 60 days of the request. If applicable law other than this act does not prohibit the custodian from complying, then the custodian must grant access to comply.[35]

Delaware was the first State to enact the

---

[35] Ibid, 24.

UFADA Act, but enactment has stalled through all other States. There has been opposition from Internet and telecommunications companies concerned that the UFADA Act raises privacy questions. Twenty-six other States have introduced legislation to enact a version of the UFADA Act during the first half of 2015, but none of those measures have been passed[36]. The adoption of the UFADA Act in Kentucky and Mississippi has been defeated, and the legislature in Colorado and Maryland have postponed considering and voted against it respectively[37].

The version of the UFADA Act enacted by Delaware has more detailed definitions of "digital asset", "digital device" and "digital account" than its parent uniform act did.

"Digital account" means an electronic system for creating,

---

[36] Morgan Weiner, 'Opposition to the Uniform Fiduciary Access to Digital Assets Act', The National Law Review (USA), 21 July 2015 < http://www.natlawreview.com/article/opposition-to-uniform-fiduciary-access-to-digital-assets-act>.

[37] States Struggle to Adopt Uniform Access to Digital Assets Act', ARMA International (USA), 8 April 2015, < (http://www.arma.org/r1/news/washington-policy-brief/2015/04/08/states-struggle-to-adopt-uniform-access-to-digital-assets-act>.

generating, sending, sharing, communicating, receiving, storing, displaying, or processing information which provides access to a digital asset which currently exists or may exist as technology develops or such comparable items as technology develops, stored on any type of digital device, regardless of the ownership of the digital device upon which the digital asset is stored, including but not limited to, email accounts, social network accounts, social media accounts, file sharing accounts, health insurance accounts, health care accounts, financial management accounts, domain registration accounts, domain name service accounts, web hosting accounts, tax preparation service accounts, online store accounts and affiliate programs thereto, and other online accounts which currently exist to may exist as technology develops or such comparable items as technology develops.

"Digital asset" means data, text, emails, documents, audio, video, images, sounds, social media content, social networking content, codes, health care records, health insurance records, computer source codes, computer programs, software, software licences, databases, or the like, including the usernames and passwords, created, generated, sent, communicated, shared, received, or stored by electronic means on a digital device.

"Digital device" means an electronic device that can create, generate, send, share, communicate, receive, store, display, or process information, and such electronic devices shall include, but not limited to, desktops, laptops, tablets, peripherals, servers, mobile telephones, smartphones, and any similar storage device which currently exists or may exist as technology develops or such comparable items as technology develops. [38]

Europe's Data Protection Directive 95/46/EC provides data subjects with certain

---

[38] An Act to Amend Title 12 of the Delaware Code Relating to Fiduciary Access to Digital Assets and Digital Accounts, 79:416 (2015).

rights to protect their privacy, and also includes the right to access personal data processed by data controllers such as Facebook. But the Data Protection Directive[39] is silent on whether it applies to deceased persons. Various countries in Europe have adopted the directive into local legislation, including the Data Protection Act 1988 in Ireland, which limits a 'data subject' to a 'living individual', meaning that the data protection law does not survive the death of a European Union account user[40].

There is no other legislation that specifically includes provisions for the succession of digital assets.

Case law

Part of the reason that there is such a reluctance to adopt the UFADA Act in the United States appears to be the strong privacy rights that dominate that jurisdiction, and that they utilise a torts and contractual model to

---

[39] Data Protection Directive 95/46/EC .

[40] Damien McCagllig, 'Facebook after death: an evolving policy in a social network' (2013) International Journal of Law and Information Technology, pp 1-34
<ijlit.oxfordjournals.org/content/early/2013/09/25/ijlit.eat012.full>, 20.

protect privacy. Conversely, European countries mainly perceive privacy and control over personal data as a human right. The United Kingdom and Australia lie somewhere in between, and a property-based model to personal data has mainly been a theoretical construction, as it has not been applied so far[41]. There has not been litigation that specifically deals with digital assets as property of a deceased estate, only whether an executor or administrator can consent to give access to digital content on behalf of a deceased. The following cases primarily deal with the privacy rights of a deceased person:

In 2005, 22-year-old Loren Williams was killed in motorbike accident in Oregon, USA. His mother Karen contacted Facebook, asking them not to delete her son's account. She then obtained his log in and password through a friend and began logging in until the password was changed (or deactivated) by Facebook. There followed a period of negotiations between Karen's lawyer and Facebook after which they agreed that Karen

---

[41] Edina Harbinja, 'Does the EU Data Protection regime protect post-mortem privacy and what could be the potential alternatives?' (2013) 10(1) Scripted <script-ed.org/wp-content/uploads/2013/04/harbinja.pdf>, 4.2.1.

could have access to Loren's account for 10 months. Consent orders to this affect were obtained from Multnomah County Circuit Court in 2007[42].

Blake Fought died in March 2007 in the Virginia Tech high school shootings. The campaign by his family, and eventually those of other slain students[43] brought about the change in Facebook's removal of profiles policy and an introduction of a permanent memorialised profile[44].

By 2008, Facebook had stopped allowing access to a deceased's account and only allowing copies of the content of the account. In England in December 2008, Sahar Daftary fell from a 12th story balcony of an apartment. Her family sought disclosure of the contents of her Facebook account covering the 20 day period prior to her death. The parties agreed that the USA Stored

---

[42] Damien McCagllig, 'Facebook after death: an evolving policy in a social network' (2013) International Journal of Law and Information Technology, pp 1-34 <ijlit.oxfordjournals.org/content/early/2013/09/25/ijlit.eat012.full>, 14.

[43] Kristina Kelleher, Facebook profiles become makeshift memorials (2007) The Brown Daily Herald <http://www.browndailyherald.com/2007/02/22/facebook-profiles-become-makeshift-memorials/> at 6 November 2015.

[44] Above, n 46, 12.

Communication Act applied to the contents of the communications in the account, but the Daftly family argued that Anisa Daftary, as administrator of Sahar's estate, was entitled to consent to the disclosure of the contents of the account and therefore fell within one of the exceptions to the Stored Communication Act[45]. Facebook argued that given the number of jurisdictions that their users span, it would be far too burdensome to require Facebook to review the law of each jurisdiction in order to confirm the extent of the powers vested in administrators and confirm if they included the power to consent in such a situation. The court determined that it couldn't compel Facebook to production records contrary to the Stored Communications Act, and that it did not have the jurisdiction to deal with the issue of lawful consent by an administrator of an estate. But the court also suggested that there was nothing stopping Facebook from voluntarily providing the materials requested[46].

Benjamin Stassen committed suicide in 2010. The family got a court order that they

---

[45] In re Request for Order Requiring Facebook, Inc to Produce Documents and Things, Case No C 12-80171 LHK (PSG) (N.D. California, 20 Sept 2012).

[46] Above, n46, 15-16.

were the heirs to their son's estate and are entitled to the contents of his Facebook account. Facebook wouldn't comply with the court order, except after lengthy negotiations, and a promise from Stassen's parents that they would never disclosure the information in the account to third parties. This case goes to show that even where an administrator of an estate does have the power to give lawful consent to the contents of a Facebook account, Facebook is still under no obligation to release those communications because the Stored Communications Act clearly grants to the provider a discretionary power of whether or not to disclose contents of communications[47].

In Brazil, the mother of Juliana Ribeiro Campos, a 24-year-old who died from complications following surgery, tried for 7 months to delete the profile of her daughter. The profile was memorialised, but the deceased's mother was distressed by the posting of messages and photos by family and friends to the deceased's page. On 19 March 2013 and again on 10 April 2013 Judge Vania de Paula Arantes issued an order for

---

[47] Ibid, 17.

Facebook to shut down the account immediately - the second order was issued with a reminder that the penalty for disobeying the court was imprisonment. Facebook did not appear or respond to the court application, and the profile was deleted.[48]

The court in Ajemian v Yahoo! adopts the principle that where the custodian online business disclaims ownership of the contents of the account, as most of those analysed in part 4 of this paper do, the appropriate forum to settle a question as to the power and authority of executors or administrators of a deceased estate over the contents of a digital account would be where the deceased was domiciled. [49]

None of the above cases have involved the situation where there was an express direction or appointment in the deceased's Will giving the executor or administrator of the estate access to digital accounts. It appears, in relation to stored information and electronic communication, that Facebook at least wants

[48] Jefferson Puff, Brazil Judge orders Facebook memorial page removed, (2013), BBC News <http://www.bbc.com/news/world-latin-america-22286569> at 16 November 2015.

[49] Ajemian v Yahoo! 12-P-178 (Massachusetts Ct App, 7 May 2013).

to hide behind the Fourth Amendment of the USA Constitution as extended and codified under the Stored Communications Act, but it is arguable that restricting a deceased's family from access digital content was not the purpose of that legislation.[50]

---

[50] Stored Communications Act, Wikipedia <https://en.wikipedia.org/wiki/Stored_Communications_Act> at 16 November 2015.

21 SUGGESTED DEFINITIONS AND PRACTICES

Assess suitable groupings

Based on analysing the social media and online businesses, their terms of use, and generally how they operate in the section above, it is clear that what we may consider to be a digital asset that we own may not be the case at all. Many of the online accounts actually have a number of elements to them, some of which can be retrieved and others that cannot. It is therefore useful to group or categorise types of online accounts and assets, so that a system can be developed for dealing with each group or category.

The following groupings or elements are considered relevant:

- Licenced use
    These kind of online accounts involve the purchase of a licence to use a piece of content or game. This licence to use is not transferrable, and is a contractual relationship that dies with the account holder. The types of online accounts included in this grouping are music, TV shows, ebooks, movies and other content on iTunes, and ebooks and magazines from Kindle. These are not an asset and will not form part of a deceased estate.

- Stored information
    Online services that allow the account holder to store their own content on the virtual server or cloud system come within this grouping. The uploaded content all belongs to the account holder; this could be photos, files, home movies, and other data. The virtual server is just like having a C drive on your computer, and you retain

ownership of all the content. You are entitled to it back when you close the account. This grouping would include services like Dropbox, Google Drive, and Evernote. This content is an asset and should be treated as such as part of a deceased estate.

- Cloud software

Cloud software is a step further than a stored information system. Cloud software is an online system for arranging and displaying or interpreting your data. It is all your own data, and you are entitled to your data back when you close your account, but you would need other software to interpret the data. This grouping would include services like accounting software Xero. The data is your asset, but the right to continuing using the software is a contractual relationship which ends with the death of the account holder. The data should be treated as part of the deceased estate once it is downloaded from the cloud software.

- Electronic communication

These are personal messages that

you send to or receive from other people. These are via email or message, whether the email is purely an email account or an internal communication mechanism within another account type, such as the messaging capability within Facebook or LinkedIn. They are not public published content, and they are not displayed in a public feed. Though not valuable in most cases, electronic communications should be treated as assets of a deceased estate, just like the diaries and love letters of a deceased is treated as part of the chattels of the deceased.

• Social media platform

These accounts are dominated by privacy rules and by the sharing of content with there users. They are also a combination of a number of the aspects of the above groupings, but need to be treated differently. There are aspects of stored information with social media accounts, particular with photo uploads. These should be considered assets and be downloadable for the estate. There are aspects of electronic communication within social media platforms, and these should also be treated as assets and recoverable by the deceased estate. Otherwise the use of the social media platform should be considered a licenced use, which terminates on the death of the account holder. Though there is some argument that there is value in the account feed of a celebrity account, it is a leap to find property in an account feed. Users of social media should have the right to say what happens to their account on death, instead of it being mandatorily closed or mandatorily memorialised - they might want to be forgotten, or they might not want to be. But if a position is not nominated by an account holder, it is difficult to say what the default position should be.

- Digital property

  These primarily consist of domain names, which are like a piece of Internet real estate, or the content of a website which has been designed and paid for like a house on a piece of real estate, particularly if the website is an e-commerce site. These should be considered assets for the purposes of a deceased estate, and transferrable. This does not include the 'ownership' of retail accounts where domain names are bought and websites are hosted. The transferree should have their own retail accounts where the domain name and the website hosting is transferred.

Define elements with a definition or classification regime

To make sense of the groups above, and to develop a language that can be utilised in either legislation or the drafting of documentation, we need to have definitions of common terms. In developing a system to deal with each of the elements or categories outlined in part 5.1 of this paper, a language of common defined terms is necessary.

The below definitions have been adapted from the UFADA Act, the Delaware version of the UFADA Act, and the *Electronic Transactions (Victoria) Act* 2000:

'Account holder' means a person that has entered into a terms-of-service agreement with a custodian.

'API' means a set of functions and procedures that allow the creation of applications which access the features or data of an operating system, application, or other service.

'Cloud software' means a model for enabling the uploading and entry of digital information into an operating system or data management system that interprets and displays the digital information for the account holder, with the source data being stored online or in a virtual server and not directly on a digital device.

'Custodian' means a person or business that electronically stores digital assets or digital accounts of an account holder or otherwise has control over digital assets or digital accounts of the account holder.

'Digital account' means an electronic system for creating, generating, sending, sharing, communicating, receiving, storing, displaying, or processing information which provides access to digital information or a digital asset which currently exist or may exist as technology develops or such comparable items as technology develops, stored on any type of digital device, regardless of the ownership of the digital device upon which the digital asset is stored, including but not limited to, email accounts, social media accounts, file sharing accounts, health insurance accounts, health care accounts, financial management accounts, domain registration accounts, domain name service accounts, web hosting accounts, tax preparation service accounts, online store accounts and affiliate program thereto, and other online accounts which currently exist or may exist as technology develops or such comparable items as technology develops.

'Digital asset' means digital information, including the usernames and passwords, created, generated, sent, communicated, shared, received or stored by electronic means in a digital account or on a digital device by an account holder.

'Digital device' means an electronic device that can create, generate, send, share, communicate, receive, store, display, or process information, and such electronic devices shall include, but not limited to, desktops, laptops, tablets, peripherals, servers, mobile telephones, smartphones, and any similar storage device which currently exists or may exist as technology develops or such comparable items as technology develops.

'Digital information' means digitised data, text, images, video, sounds, codes, computer programs, software, databases, and facts and information about the account holder, interactive electronic content, or the like.

'Digital property' means a intellectual property rights in electronic format, including a registered domain name, and website design and website content relating to a registered domain name, or hosted by a custodian for an account holder.

'Electronic communication' means any transfer of signs, signals, writing, images, sounds, data, or intelligence of any nature transmitted in whole or in part by a wire, radio, electromagnetic, photoelectronic or photo-optical system that is personal in nature or affects local or international commerce.

'Licenced use' means an account holder being contractually licensed by the custodian to personally use digital information owned or created by a third party which the custodian has rights to licence account holders for a fee.

'Social media platform' means a set of APIs, websites and services (such as content) that enable account holders, including application developers and website operators, upload content and interact with other account holders.

'Stored information' means digital information that has been uploaded from a digital device via a to an online or virtual server allocated to a digital account of an account holder.

'Uploaded content' means digital information that the account holder submits or posts to the Internet, or that third parties submit or post about the account holder, to provide or share in a digital account.

Categorise social media and online businesses

As outlined earlier, many of the digital accounts analysed have multiple elements. Each of the elements needs an individual system for the executor of a deceased estate to deal with the underlying digital information. The elements are more important than the online business or custodian itself. Similarly, the terms and conditions of the digital accounts determine what elements are involved, and therefore what system should be utilised by the executor.

The following table is merely a demonstration of the elements the make up each of the digital account types already analysed. Using a similar process, all forms of digital account can have the elements broken down, and then the relevant system for each element can be applied:

Online business	Licenced use	Stored information	Cloud software	Electronic communication	Social media platform	Digital property
iTunes	X					
Google	X	X	X	X	X	
Hotmail/Microsoft	X	X	X	X		

Online business	Lice nced use	Stored infor matio n	Cloud softw are	Electr onic comm unicat ion	Social media platfo rm	Digita l prope rty
Facebo ok		X		X	X	
Twitter		X		X	X	
eBay	X			X		X
Flickr		X			X	
Paypal	X					
Dropb ox		X				
Linked In		X		X	X	
Pintere st		X			X	
Skype	X			X		
Instagr am		X			X	
Kindle /Amaz	X					

Online business	Licenced use	Stored information	Cloud software	Electronic communication	Social media platform	Digital property
on						
Evernote		X				
Domain name						X
Website hosting	X					

It should be noted that other elements can also form part of a custodian's online business, such as a Facebook business Page, which is different from an individual's profile, could be digital property that can be transferred can changing the administrator of the Page.

iTunes accounts, FlyBuys accounts and PayPal accounts are merely a licensed use, and there should not be any expectation of any ongoing benefit from these accounts. There will be a specific methodology or system developed for dealing with licensed use accounts which should be followed for digital accounts with this element. Digital accounts that have an element of stored information, such as Facebook, DropBox and Evernote, should allow for the download or retrieval of all the stored information. There will also be a specific methodology or system developed for dealing with stored information that can be applied to this element within any digital account. Similarly, those digital accounts with an element of digital property, such as a domain name, will have a specific methodology or system for dealing with that element of the digital account.

Propose a standard practice for each element

The purpose of this book is not to argue that certain types of accounts should not be a mere licensed use, for example. The purpose of this paper is to deal with the custodians and the elements of their digital accounts under the terms of agreement that currently exist. Outlined below is a standard approach for each of the elements listed previously, and what can be expected to be recovered for each element:

- Licensed use

    As noted above, an element of a digital account that is a licensed used is not an asset and will not form part of the deceased estate, no matter how much money was spent by the deceased accumulating content in the account. The practical approach is to download all the content via the deceased's own account, such as music data files or ebooks, onto a digital device that can be continued to be used by the beneficiaries of the estate. Those digital files cannot be transferred to another account or device linked to another account. The account should then be closed.

- Stored information

    Digital accounts with this element include digital information that belongs to the deceased account holder that is merely stored by a custodian. The executor of the estate should contact the custodian with proof of death and proof of authority, and then the stored information should be provided. The request by the executor should seek a copy of the content of the account, being the stored information. The executor may be given temporary access to the account to download the digital information, or the custodian may send the executor a digital device with the digital information on it.

- Cloud software

    The approach for digital information stored within cloud software should be the same as that for the element of stored information. The executor of the estate should contact the custodian with the request, and the custodian will provide the digital information in return. Often this digital information will not be readable unless formatted by software, so the executor may have to consider how to recreate the information into a readable format.

- Electronic communication

    These are all the private messages to and from the deceased account holder. Similar again to stored information and cloud software, the executor should contact the custodian with the request, and the custodian should provide the digital information in return.

- Social media platform

    It should be made clear to an executor that any social media platform will contain other elements which can be recovered. However, how the profile and feed on the platform is dealt with after the death of the account holder is determined by the contract between the custodian and the account holder. Unless a direction has been expressly made by the deceased account holder tin their account, the custodian can decide. The executor will usually not be able to dictate to the custodian what should be done, but should notify the custodian and not just leave the account active.

- Digital property

    Digital property forms part of the deceased estate and is transferrable to beneficiaries or can be sold. Domain name registrars can transfer domains, and website hosts can transfer website content to beneficiaries. These can also be sold for value. Similarly, an eBay store, or Facebook Page can be transferred by changing the administrator details.

Practical aspects of practice

During administration, a list of digital accounts should be compiled, just like one would with other estate assets, and consider an approach for each. Using the elements outlined, a solicitor could decide which elements comprise each digital account, and then know what is likely to be recovered and how.

The initial contact with each of the custodians of the digital accounts is usually done online. With Facebook, for example, only a Friend of the deceased can notify Facebook of a death. So a solicitor cannot use their own Facebook account to notify of a death unless they are already a Friend of the deceased. Practically, solicitors should be aware that if an executor needs assistance with the initial notifications, then they will need to have access to a laptop, personal computer or tablet in the firm's office to be guided to their accounts.

With enough hunting through the Help or

Support sections of each custodian's website, one can discover a physical address for correspondence. This would allow a solicitor to then take a more traditional approach as with a bank or other service provider, and send an initial letter to the custodian with a certified copy of a death certificate and copy of a Will to initiate the notification process.

Just like with different banks, it should be expected that each custodian would have a different requirement for proof of death and different forms that need to be completed. Each will have a different policy for dealing with the death of an account holder, and this is not something to fear, but to manage.

During the estate planning process, it is still relevant to advise clients to leave a list of their digital accounts and passwords, or they could sign up for password software where all passwords are stored with one master password. If the executor has the usernames and passwords, they could access some of the accounts and download digital content prior to contacting the custodian. However, this does not remove the requirement to notify the custodian since it is the executor's duty to collect in assets and close accounts.

Difficulties will continue to arise in cases where there is no express guidance in a deceased's Will about such accounts, or whilst the powers of executors and administrators in relation to digital accounts remains unclear in legislation. The executor may struggle to prove to the custodian that they have authority over the digital account of the deceased account holder unless there is an express provision in a Will, or they obtain a court order to that affect.

The resistance to the adoption of the UFADA Act has also been noted in the USA, and it is proposed that the resistance arises because that Act adopts an opt-out approach rather than an opt-in approach. The custodians appear to require confirmation that the deceased account holder has expressly considered what would happen to their accounts when they die and to expressly confer power on their nominee. It is for these reasons that this paper does not recommend that legislation similar to the UFADA Act be introduced to Australia.

Whether there is legislation introduced or not, it is recommended that solicitors turn their mind to drafting definitions and executor powers for their clients, and to review their precedents to include such definitions and clauses as standard.

The goal during the estate planning process should be to actually discuss the digital estate with the clients, rather than to gloss over it, so it should be added to any checklist that is used during an interview. Clearly, if standard clauses and powers are not sufficient for the client's objectives, and individual accounts needs to be dealt with separately with specific instructions, then unique clauses need to be drafted or a statement of wishes could be prepared to accompany the Will.

Some tips for digital estate planning

- make sure you use definitions in your estate planning documents
- draft a clause in the power of attorney authorising the attorn to access, use, delete, control or transfer any part of the digital estate
- draft a clause in the will authorising the executor to access, use, delete, control, transfer, distribute or dispose of any part of the digital estate

• draft a memorandum of wishes for the attorney and/or executor with instructions on the digital estate and how it is to the dealt with

• have clients complete an inventory of their digital estate, and obtain details where the updated version will be kept. Don't take the inventory and passwords due to the security risk. Place a record with the will (not in the will) of where the inventory holding the details is stored is the best option

Some tips for digital estate administration

• making an inventory of the deceased's known digital estate, including contact lists, email accounts and social media accounts

• find people who have the appropriate technical and legal knowledge to access the digital estate

• if it is necessary, change passwords

• consider what form the digital devices should be given to the beneficiaries

• consider whether it is prudent to buy an external hard drive and copy all data and store it all in a secure place

• consider how access to each digital

account is regulated and how to notify the custodian

- consider what needs to be done with the digital accounts - whether they should be deleted, transferred, sold, downloaded, memorialised, or cashed-out
- take steps to protect the privacy of the deceased person, and
- inform the relevant custodians that the account user has died.

22 PRECEDENT CLAUSES

Standard trustee power

In addition to all other powers conferred by law my executors may in their discretion exercise the power to access, use, delete or control my digital accounts including but not limited to Facebook, iTunes, [list other important accounts] to download, transfer, delete, distribute, copy, duplicate, or otherwise deal with my digital information in my digital accounts and I hereby authorise and direct the custodian of my digital accounts to provide my executors with my usernames and passwords to enable access.

Specific trustee power

In addition to all other powers conferred by law my executors have the power and are directed to access and delete my [specific digital account] and all its content [is to be deleted/downloaded] prior to deletion and I hereby authorise and direct the custodian of my [specific digital account] to provide my executors with my username and password to enable access and to directly delete my account at the expiration of 6 months from providing such username and password to my executors if they have not deleted it themselves.

Bequest of specific digital device and contents

I give my [eg. Kindle device and its contents] to [beneficiary name] absolutely.

Bequest of digital information

I give all my digital information contained in any digital device or held by any custodian in a digital account, including but not limited to Facebook, Dropbox, [list other important accounts] to [beneficiary name] absolutely.

Precatory trust

I give my digital information contained in my [eg. Evernote account] to [beneficiary name] (in this clause called "the Donee") and without imposing any trust or legal obligation upon the Donee so to do I desire that the Donee will [eg. compile my notes for my final novel into a form that can be published for the benefit of my estate].

Domain name

I give my domain name and website known at the date of this will as [domain name], or if I do not own this domain name at the date of my death then such other domain name that my business [business name] is run from, to [beneficiary name].

ABOUT THE AUTHOR

Jacqui Brauman is the principal solicitor of TBA Law. She has a Bachelor of Laws, Bachelor of Accounting, Advanced Diploma in Taxation Law, and a Masters in Applied Law (Wills and Estates).

Practicing mainly in wills and estates, and property law, Jacqui's career of nearly 10 years has taken her from Central Victoria to rural New South Wales, to Sydney, and back to the outskirts of Melbourne.

Jacqui's primary focus in her wills and estate practice is to make sure young families know the consequences of not undertaking proper planning, and ensuring that their children are adequately protected, both physically and financially. Her message is simple: In a world of uncertainty, we cannot live with our heads in the sand. Instead, we can make sure that we don't leave a difficult mess behind us if something should happen. Then, hopefully, the plan never has to be implemented. But it's better to plan for security than try to struggle during grief and loss.

More recently, with the increasing use of the Internet and social media, Jacqui has developed a keen interest in digital assets and how to deal with them in estate plans, or as part of the administration of a deceased estate.

Public school educated and raised in Wangaratta, Jacqui is married to Daniel Brauman who is a serving member in the Royal Australian Army. This live together with their blue-heeler at their property just south of Seymour. Together they do plenty of adventurous sports, including motorcycling, kayaking, camping, 4x4 and fishing. Jacqui also enjoys distance running and generally keeping fit.